with best wishes
Herbert Levy

Voices from the Past is the autobiography of a German Jew who was born in Berlin just three years before Hitler came to power. Herbert Levy describes vividly his experiences as he grew up in an increasingly anti-Semitic environment. As conditions worsened, so his family's efforts to escape became more and more frantic. Eventually he was put on a train, a child alone, and sent to Holland. Thence he boarded a ship for Harwich and from there travelled to London.

Later Herbert's parents were able to join him and together they experienced the privations and horrors of the Blitz, but not before he and his mother had been separated from his father and interned on the Isle of Man. The war at last over, he found himself in the ironic position of being called up for National Service in the British Army.

Voices from the Past is a vividly told tale and an impassioned plea that we should never allow ourselves to forget.

Herbert Levy was born in Berlin but, as a child, fled Nazi Germany and came to England where he was eventually joined by his parents. He experienced evacuation from London, internment as an alien in a camp on the Isle of Man and, ironically, National Service as a British soldier in the Royal Army Education Corps.

He worked with the English National Opera at Sadler's Wells for several years and has broadcast often on the World Service.

As well as writing plays for children, he has directed several productions including *Joseph and his Amazing Technicolour Dreamcoat*.

Married with two children, he is now a volunteer guide with the Anne Frank Travelling Exhibition.

D1076637

VOICES FROM THE PAST

Herbert Levy

Temple House Books
Sussex, England

The Book Guild Ltd,
25 High Street,
Lewes, Sussex

First published 1995
© Herbert Levy 1995
Paperback edition 1995
Reprinted 1998
Reprinted 2000
Set in Baskerville
Typesetting by Ashford Setting & Design Services
Ashford, Middlesex
Printed in Great Britain by
Athenæum Press Ltd,
Gateshead, Tyne & Wear

A catalogue record for this book is
available from the British Library

ISBN 1 85776 087 5

CONTENTS

For Andrew, Hilary and Mike
so that they should not forget.

For Lilian
who helped me to remember.

1

EARLY DAYS

Many German Jews of an older generation than mine still have some happy memories of Germany despite the Nazi period. I suppose they remember the times before Hitler came to power. When he did become Chancellor I was only three years old. What I remember of that time, young as I was, is solely connected with what was done to the Jews and how they were treated.

The harassment of the Jews started almost immediately. I still vividly remember being woken in the middle of the night when I was only three or four years old. There was a heavy knocking at the front door. Six or seven Brown Shirts (S.A. men) dressed in their uniforms stood there. They demanded immediate entry. They had been told to find the illegal Communist propaganda that we were hiding. The Communist Party had been banned by then. However, my father had never been a member of the Communist or any other political party. The men searched the whole flat thoroughly. After a long time they left having not found any illegal literature. What, however, my father found next morning was that his wallet containing a considerable amount of money had disappeared. When the police were contacted about this they were unhelpful.

The racial laws were soon enforced. There was a whole

new study called *Rassenkunde,* a science to be learned by pupils at school. There are still photos in existence, taken at schools in those days. Jewish children are paraded at the front of the class. Here the pupils were instructed in this 'science'. They were told one could tell quite clearly by the lips, the shape of the head, the colour of the hair and the eyes who was a member of the Aryan Super Race and who belonged to inferior categories. Later on Jewish children could only attend a Jewish school. I myself went to a state school for two terms only and had to be very careful how I behaved there. For the third term of my first scholastic year I was transferred to a Jewish school.

It was at about this time that my aunt took a photo of me (a four-year old) and my thirteen-year old schoolgirl cousin, Ellen-Eva, who happened to have long plaits of golden hair. My aunt took the roll of film to be developed at a local shop. Soon afterwards we saw a huge enlargement of this photograph of the two of us in the shop window. For a number of weeks the enlargement travelled around Berlin and was shown in other photographic shop windows. The caption underneath read 'Two Beautiful Aryan Children'. I don't know whether we were beautiful, but we certainly were not aryan. It was very lucky for us no-one ever realised the mistake that had been made. However, it does go to prove how absurd this new science of race really was.

In 1936 the Olympic Games took place in Berlin at the special *Sportspalast.* People flocked from all over the world to watch these Games. No-one seemed concerned at the events that were happening in that city to Jews, gypsies, homosexuals and other 'inferior' people at the same time. Not one competing nation thought it proper to boycott these games. Some foreign contestants even gave the Nazi salute. Eventually, when Hitler refused to shake hands with the very successful US athlete, Jesse Owens, no-one seemed to mind. Jesse Owens, of course, belonged to the inferior black race and was therefore unworthy to have won four gold medals.

One afternoon during this summer of 1936 my mother took me to the park, the *Tiergarten*. Jews were still allowed into parks at that time. The day wore on and it was time to go home. As we left by our usual route, we came towards a wide avenue. A crowd of people had gathered there. As soon as my mother saw this she tried to turn back. It was always wise to avoid crowds at this time. But it was too late.

One of the people grabbed hold of me, saying to my mother 'Give us the child so he can see the *Fuehrer*'.

Without much ceremony I was lifted into the air and passed over the heads of the people to the very front. In later years, at London football matches, I often saw this happening in order to give little boys a better view of the match. This time it was very frightening for both my mother and me. Apparently Hitler in his limousine was expected to pass here on his way back from the day's Olympic events.

Shortly afterwards I began to hear the gradually increasing shouts of 'Heil Hitler' as the car slowly approached and Hitler acknowledged the adulation of the crowd. What was I to do? Even as a six-year-old I realised I could be in trouble. I knew the many bad things Hitler and his Nazi party had done to the Jews. On the other hand to let the crowd know that I was Jewish would at the very least cause my mother and me to be badly manhandled. I had only a very short time to come to a decision as the car drew nearer. Hearing all these shouts of 'Heil Hitler' around me, I felt I had to join in. I raised my hand and shouted with the rest of them. I am sure my mother was very grateful to me and felt relieved as I was handed back to her. We quickly left the scene.

There were almost daily events. People shouting and spitting at me on my way to school. Jewish schoolchildren had slightly different term times and therefore went to school when others did not.

It was high time to get out of Germany. But it was almost impossible to get entry visas to other countries. By the time I was eight I knew the name of every South American country and its capital. I knew that Shanghai was in China. This was not because I was such a good pupil at Geography. I had heard my parents and their friends discussing time after time the most likely and the most unlikely places where they might have a chance of entry. I was always told never to mention anything that had been discussed at home. I heeded this warning well and I know I never betrayed their trust.

At times it seemed utterly hopeless and more was to come in 1938 with *Kristallnacht*.

2

MISHPOCHOLOGY

In Yiddish the term for relatives is *Mishpoche*. There is even a Yiddish saying which, roughly translated, means 'It's O.K. to have relatives as long as one doesn't have to bother too much with them'. Jews generally bother a lot with family. My mother was a great expert on family relationships and family trees. She even discovered that my wife and I were related – our relationship is similar to that of Queen Elizabeth and Prince Philip. Like them, we have a mutual great-great-grandmother. My mother almost made a study or a science of it, so that we called it *Mishpochology*. My wife and I and our children listened to her with fascination. Unfortunately, we never got her to write anything down, so that a lot of all this is lost. That is why I have decided in various essays to write something of our more immediate history. I am now the last of my generation of my mother's family. In fact there are no more Steins (my mother's maiden name). So I am the only one who can remember anything about us during the Nazi period.

I do not know a lot about my father's family, because I saw them seldom, unlike my mother's parents, whom I saw daily while I lived in Berlin. My grandfather Salomon Levy (whose Hebrew name I was given) was born in 1871 and died in 1923 before I was born. I believe his death was due to injuries he received during the First World War when he served in the German army. The whole family came from the southern part of Germany. In fact they originally came from Alsace and part of the family remained there after the 1914-18 war, when the territory was returned to France, and thus became French citizens. This was to prove useful during the Second World War, when grandmother Levy was sent to a German concentration camp in France. Through efforts of her French relatives she was released from the camp in Gurs after a time and was able to spend the rest of the war relatively unmolested in Lourdes, which was then part of Vichy France.

My father Arthur, as well as his older brother and two younger sisters were born in a small town called Hockenheim, in the county of Baden. It is famous now for its motor racing track. The Levy family had a wholesale paint business, which my grandmother carried on after the death of her husband. The elder brother was taken into the firm but not my father Arthur. There was some sort of disagreement. My father left home for Berlin. There he met my mother, Rose Stein. They were married in August, 1927.

It is a common joke among Jews that everyone's grand-father always seems to have been a Rabbi. My grandfather Stein's grandfather really was a Rabbi. Some long time ago their name had been Jerushalmi and they had come from Palestine to Hungary where my grandfather Phillip was born. His father, Samuel Stein, seems to have been an odd man. He was a free-thinker who on Saturday nights, when the Sabbath seemed to last too long, just drew the curtains and said it was dark now, so the Sabbath was over. He lived to a ripe old age, and died in his 91st year on 27th May, 1916.

My grandfather Phillip was born on 8th June, 1853 in Hungary, the oldest of four brothers. I still remember a portrait painting of the four brothers that hung in my grandparents' apartment in Berlin. The whole Stein clan seems to have been intellectuals and thus usually hard up.

My grandmother Henrietta (Jettchen) née Joseph came from a more wealthy family. Her father, Josef Joseph, born in Filehne in 1831, went to America when he was about fifteen to seek his fortune. He seems to have succeeded, though not without tragedy. He was a trader who travelled around the country supplying frontiersmen in very far-off places. Being successful, Josef sent off home for his teenage brother Isaac to come and join him in America to help him in his business. One day in 1858 this young brother Isaac was ambushed in Hartford, robbed and killed. The older brother found him dead on the road. There was a letter – now lost – that he sent to his parents, telling of this dreadful event, apologising to his parents and blaming himself for not having watched better over his younger brother. I have heard this story told, but I also found details of it in correspondence between my grandmother in Germany and my uncle Org in New York, before the United States had entered the war. In order to give my grandmother a better chance of being admitted to the States they were desperately trying to establish that her father, Josef, had become a US citizen. Alas, all to no avail.

This Josef Joseph returned from America a relatively wealthy man, bought property and married my great-grandmother, Jeanette Lachmann (born 1st January, 1842, died 1st January, 1913). They had three daughters of whom my grandmother Jettchen was the oldest. Her father died in 1879 before she was ten years old and her mother was a widow with three small children when she was still in her thirties.

My grandmother was born on 13th December, 1869, so she was sixteen years younger than my grandfather. I don't know how they met, but they were married in Berlin, Heidereuter Gasse Synagogue on 26th December, 1889. Despite their age difference it was a very happy marriage. They were great opposites. My grandfather was the intellectual. Recently, on a visit to Israel, I was shown a poem in German composed by someone at a family function during the 1890s. All the four brothers are mentioned. My grandfather is referred to as '*Phillip der Gelehrte*' – Phillip the learned one. He was very talented. We have a picture of his hanging in our study. It was painted by him when he was eighteen years old in 1872 and was exhibited in Hungary. It shows a number of flowers catalogued according to the Linné system. He also played the violin, he was a linguist and he was a wonderful speaker. On family occasions he was always asked to speak. His son Josef (Uncle Joszi) still recalled in old age, and could recite from memory, the speech his father had written for him on the occasion of his Barmitzvah about *Josef und sein Bunter Rock* – Joseph and his coat of many colours.

My grandmother was a much more light-hearted person, who enjoyed any kind of music. Whatever crisis might have come up in her life, she had the kind of temperament that could get over anything by laughing at it. All their children – and they had five of them – spoke of their parents and the home the parents provided for them with love and affection. They had three children in quick succession: Charlotte (1891), Josef (1892) and Leopold (1893).

My uncle Poldi was only a few weeks old when the Stein family left Berlin for London. They lived there for a number of years and my mother, Rose, was born there in 1900. While they lived in London my grandfather attended a meeting at which Theodor Herzl spoke. In later years he would say what a powerful speaker Herzl was. My grandfather became a convinced Zionist from that day on.

I think grandmother Joseph was anxious to see her latest granddaughter and persuaded the Steins to return to Germany. However that may have been, my mother was only eighteen months old when the Steins came back to Germany. All the four children only spoke English. When they saw a sign up in Dresden, where they first went to live, reading *Feuer Wache* (Fire Station) they read it as *Für Wäsche* (For Laundry). My mother who, at eighteen months did not yet speak fluently, had a vocabulary of only a few words. Much loved as she was by her children and grandchildren, they all felt that in later years her English vocabulary had not increased that much, although she had been born within the sound of the Bow Bells and was thus a true cockney. Her two older brothers later reported that whilst still living in Stoke Newington, London, she used to sit on the front door step and call out to them, 'Am I!'

The parents' fifth child, Georg, was born in Dresden in 1903. Soon after the whole family returned to Berlin where Grandmother Joseph had acquired a newly built corner house. This consisted of about thirty flats at the corner of Oldenburger and Union Streets. She herself had an apartment in Oldenburger Strasse and family Stein moved into a flat in Union Strasse. After a time, with a growing family, they took an additional flat in the house for the three growing boys.

Grandmother Joseph seems to have been very economically minded – certainly as far as her grandchildren were concerned. For tea parties she bought very expensive cake. However on top of the plate she put rather cheaper products costing only a few pence. These were intended for the children who were invited to take from the top. This the children were reluctant to do; sometimes they managed to grab one piece of cake from below much to the annoyance of the grandmother.

My grandfather Phillip's brother, Iszo, married my grandmother's sister Johanna – that is two brothers married two sisters. Iszo and Johanna had two daughters, Gisa and Margot, but there were no grandchildren. My grandmother's other sister, Cecilia, married an Alex Becker and they had three children. Phillip's third brother, Lajos, was a bit of a lad, it seems. He may have had children, but who is to know? The fourth brother stayed in Hungary; he had three children but only one grandson.

I remember my grandparents and their home very well, because I spent so much of my early life with them. Whenever their children or their children's friends talked about them it was always with respect and love. My uncle Joszi was an actor, his wife Hanna an opera singer. Many of their colleagues, especially when they were 'resting', often found their way to my grandparents and were always sure of a great welcome and a good meal. My grandparents enjoyed the company of artists.

My mother and uncle Org were, of course, much younger than the other three siblings. They were still children when the others were already grown up. While her brother Joszi was still at acting school my mother, a young girl, was taken by her parents to a student performance.

She enjoyed the play and when she saw her brother on the stage she excitedly shouted out for everyone to hear 'Look, there's Joszi'.

Later, when Joszi was already appearing in seasons in the provinces, he could look forward to visits from his youngest brother. Org, who was still at school, took the earliest opportunity, once his holidays had started, to seek out whatever provincial town Joszi was appearing in that year. He was always welcomed by his older brother and naturally all the other actors in the company made a great fuss of him.

During the First World War my mother's two older brothers, as British citizens, were confined in the German internment camp at *Ruhleben*. They had thus 'suffered' for Britain and were allowed to retain their British citizenship, unlike other members of the family. This was to prove life-saving for them both in the years to come.

As I said, my grandparents' place was always open house to visitors. Even I can remember the Seder nights at Passover, when a very long table was filled not only with family but with many friends as well. Until I was old enough to do it, my cousin Ellen-Eva, who was nine years older than I, asked the special four questions that have to be spoken by the youngest member around the table. Later on I said this, the *Ma Nishtanah*. All this of course stopped once the Nazis got into power.

My grandmother Levy together with her brother Julius Hirsch and his wife Paula were taken to the German concentration camp of Gurs in France. Happily they survived. Shortly after the war they were able to join their children in New York. My grandmother went straight from

France to New York to her daughter, Irma. Thus my father never got to see his mother again. She died in New York in 1958. I was lucky enough to visit New York in 1957 and as an adult met my grandmother again after nearly twenty years.

Julius and Paula Hirsch, however, went via London. They stayed with us for a couple of days to await the departure of their ship for New York. Some other relatives visited them while they were with us. The Hirschs asked for news of distant cousins called Dreifuss. They were told that sadly the parents had died in Belsen. However, their little girl had miraculously survived, been brought to London and had been adopted by a doctor's family. Years later, through correspondence my mother had with Aunt Paula, we realised that my wife Lilian was that very girl.

(See Family Tree - page 122.)

3

BIG JOURNEY FOR A LITTLE BOY

The ninth of November, 1938, was a fateful day for Jews in Germany. A lot happened and there were numerous consequences for many people. Now we know this day or rather night as *Kristallnacht* – Crystal Night – night of the shattered or of the broken glass, because the windows of Jewish shops were all broken. The synagogues were burned and destroyed. Sacred objects of Jews, including Torah scrolls and books were burned. Heinrich Heine's prediction took its first steps to becoming reality: 'The nation that burns books will end up burning people'.

To a nine-year-old like myself there were a number of repercussions. My parents' flat was the adjoining one to that of my grandparents. We spent a lot of time with them, especially as my 85-year-old grandfather had been bedbound for some time and was too frail to get up. My mother helped my aged grandmother to look after him. My parents and I were therefore with them when the Nazis turned up next day to arrest him and take him to a concentration camp. It was hopeless even trying to get him out of bed.

They therefore turned to my father and asked, 'Are you the son?' 'No, the son-in-law,' he replied. Surprisingly, they left without either one of them.

However, we had been warned. My father left immediately, making his way to my Uncle Poldi in another part of Berlin. My uncle was a British passport holder and therefore his apartment was a safe house from our point of view. Other people, not so fortunate in having relatives with foreign passports, travelled for days on the underground. Eventually the Nazis decided to check the identities of all travellers during their journey.

My mother and I moved in with my grandparents and stayed with them for several weeks. We never went to our place and I do not know whether anyone ever came there to arrest my father. The only thing I do remember was that some ashes and possibly worse had been pushed through the letter box into the hallway, probably by some kind neighbour in the house with whom we had been living on friendly terms for many years. We had noticed over the years how attitudes towards us had gradually but steadily changed. From the outright staring through us to the crossing to the other side of the street or the brief nod that it was hoped no one else would notice.

Another consequence was that after some months I managed to get out of Germany. This was quite a triumph because, although at this time every Jew was free to leave Germany, it was very difficult to get into a free country. The Swiss became quite famous for returning illegal Jewish refugees to Germany.

My family had tried for years to leave Germany but the difficulties were enormous. Every country had to issue an entry visa, which would only be granted if someone in that country would guarantee that the immigrant would not become a charge to the state – in fact that the guarantor would provide for the immigrant who, of course, was not allowed to work for his food. Even with such a guarantee many countries had quota systems.

America is a case in point. They used a quota system according to each person's country of birth. This certainly was the case in 1938. It played havoc with any immigration plans in our family. My mother was born in London. As therefore of 'British' origin her quota number was 14. She could have gone to the USA, providing she had a guarantee, straightaway. My father, however, with a similar guarantee, would not be allowed to enter the land of the free until 1941 because he was born in Germany and his number on the quota system did not come for another three years. As for my grandmother, her case was even more hopeless.

She was born in the last century in Filehne in what was then Germany. This however was changed after the First World War and Filehne became part of Poland. Thus she was on the Polish quota which was not only small but had many more applicants. So her quota number would become due in about 1950. Obviously British people were more welcome in the USA than Poles.

However, after the 9th November, 1938, the situation changed slightly – for children. The British Government relented somewhat. They decided to let in 10,000 children – all of course having guarantees from private individuals or from Jewish organisations in Britain. These 10,000 children represented about one tenth of children's applications. My parents decided to send me to safety, having obtained, through my Uncle Joszi, who was in London, a guarantee from a Mme Deveau, a lady I was destined never to meet.

These were the *Kindertransporte* : parts of trains in various parts of Germany were taken over by Jewish organisations, filled with these children up to the age of sixteen and escorted to (for most of them) an uncertain future in Great Britain. These journeys took place regularly from the end of 1938 until July, 1939. It is said that thus 10,000 Jewish children were saved. Strictly this is not quite true, for according to Hitler's Nazi Race Laws anyone who had one Jewish grandparent was considered Jewish. So little children, whose parents were Christian, who had been baptised and brought up as Christians, who knew nothing about Jews and who may even until quite lately have been members of the Hitler Youth, would suddenly find themselves considered as being Jewish. These were also among the 10,000.

All these things are in the distant past, yet I remember them well. The Jewish school I attended gradually losing more and more of its pupils – those lucky enough to be able to emigrate. My way to school was a long one. I did not live in a Jewish district and therefore my walk to school from quite an early age was several miles. Friends were also difficult – none of my fellow pupils lived anywhere near me. I therefore had to make friends locally. Boys refused to associate with me – except for one who said he would stick by me and never, never join the Hitler Youth. This is where I learnt my first lesson in organising youth groups: if they are reluctant, give them jobs with titles. This boy was approached, persuaded to accept an office with a title and in no time at all he became a fervent member of the Nazi organisation.

There was a small café on the ground floor of our house which served drinks and hot meals mostly to regular customers. We, of course, knew the owners for many years. They had a son a few years younger than I. Nevertheless I used to go in there quite often to play with him. In fact, despite our age difference, we got on quite well together. One day, however, the mother came up to me, rather shamefaced, and asked me not to come any more as some customers had objected to my being there and had threatened no longer to patronise the café.

As I left for the last time I clearly heard someone saying 'There is an awful smell of garlic suddenly'.

My friends were therefore few. Some of the girls in our street still deigned to play with me: girls are softer than boys. The friends I made at school became fewer. What happened to those Jewish children who remained behind I dare not think.

At this time it was no longer possible for Jews to go to the cinema or any other place of entertainment. Any kind of relaxation for a little Jewish boy was therefore most difficult. On Sundays there was always a small fairground open on a meadow some miles away from us. For some strange reason that I still cannot understand Jews were not excluded here. I therefore often spent Sunday afternoons there. Each ride cost 10 Pfennigs. There were so many attractions. I used to go there clutching my 10 Pfennig, excited with anticipation on which one of these I would spend the money that afternoon. The choice was enormous: there were swings, carousels, big wheels, bumper cars. Best of all there was a variety show inside a tent. I already had a passion for acting and anything connected with the theatre. So it was always a big decision which one I would choose and I managed to ring the changes over the weeks.

The time came for me to join the *Kindertransport* for London. It was the final Sunday before I left and it was the last time I would visit this palace of entertainment. Because it was my last visit I was given 50 Pfennigs. Can you imagine the unadulterated happiness I felt: with these riches I would be able to participate in all these varied events.

Full of joy I left home. Nearby I met two of the girls who lived near us and who were among the ones that still used to play with me. I believe they knew I would be leaving Berlin within a few days. They decided to accompany me to the fairground. Unfortunately, they had no money of their own, so they had to watch me enjoying myself. The first go was on the Big Wheel – my first 10 Pfennigs worth. I can still remember the wheel slowly swinging to the top and as I looked down I saw far below two sad faces staring at me. At that moment I realised I had to alter my long thought-out plan and to adjust it to accommodate these two. So the three of us went on the roundabout next – a full 30 Pfennigs worth at one go. I hope they realised in later life that Jews are not as miserly as they are often made out to be. My last 10 Pfennigs were of course spent on the Variety Show.

And so the day of my departure arrived, when I would leave my parents and my grandparents. It was early in the morning. I went next door to my grandparents' apartment to say goodbye to them. My grandfather was now 86 years old and terminally ill in bed. He was to die within a few weeks. I still remember only a year or so previously, how he used often to meet me half way on my walk back from school. When the weather was warm enough he used to buy me an ice cream. I said goodbye to him now. And my grandmother was there too. She was usually such a happy person and so proud of me. In years past she had held regular meetings with 'girls' in her class from their time at school in the previous century. I would always be called in and proudly shown off as her grandson.

My parents and I left them and downstairs in the street I can still remember my grandmother standing on that long balcony, waving to me as we three walked to the station. She waved until we were out of sight. That was also the last time I saw her.

Due to the vagaries of the US system of immigration, she was one of the six million Jews who perished in the extermination camps, together with her two sisters, many nieces, nephews and numerous cousins.

My father carried my suitcase – it was only a little one because it had to be of such a size that I could manage it on my own. It therefore could only contain the barest essentials. We took the *Stadtbahn* to the mainline terminal. Parents were not allowed on the platform. We said a quick farewell. I am totally astonished now how calm I was. The thought that I might never see my parents again never occurred to me. The children were quickly grouped together and marched to the waiting train. I can still remember how excited I was. I talked to my companion next to me, whom I had never seen before, telling him how my Uncle Joszi had written to me from London that one of his acquaintances, who had a car – a very rare possession at that time – had promised to drive us to a place called 'Seaside' one Sunday.

Although the train would leave from the main terminal it did have another stop in Berlin at Charlottenburg. My parents knew this and they rushed away to the platform at this station, so they could catch a last glimpse of their son. I have a photo in front of me now, that they took at that

23

time. I am seen, little as I was, hardly reaching the window, happily smiling because I had seen my parents. But there were several boys behind me anxiously searching the platform trying to find their parents.

I was the youngest, not yet ten, in our compartment – all boys. I remember my mother asking one of the 'big' boys – still under sixteen – to look after me; something I objected to. So this was the fourth goodbye this morning – the second one to my parents.

It was a long journey from Berlin to the Hook of Holland and then across the sea to Harwich. Money was restricted. Jewish adults could only take out 10 Reichmark (an equivalent of approximately £25 at today's prices). No valuables or jewellery of any kind could be taken. Children could not even do that. All they were allowed to take was one RM (i.e. 100 Pfennigs). This money however had to be spent on the train for drinks and suchlike. It had to be spent inside Germany. Not one Pfennig was allowed to be taken across the border. This had been carefully instilled into me. And even as a nine-year-old I had a good idea of what could be done to me if I was found to have any money on me once we came to the German border. I remember it well, because as we neared the border, I suddenly realised I still had something like 15 Pfennigs left. I was very frightened, so I took these few small coins and threw them out of the window. Recently I heard from a lady who used to be one of the adults accompanying the *Kindertransporte*, that these adult leaders used to collect any leftover coins at the border and give them to local charity.

We had been told that at the border station anyone who had reached his tenth birthday had to leave the train with his case to have it examined by the customs authorities; this was to make sure that nothing forbidden would be taken across the border. All the other boys decided they would stay put until they were asked to leave the train. We waited anxiously for a long time. We heard a lot of movement, many people on the platform. However, no-one came to our compartment and suddenly our train started up again.

24

We crossed the border and reached safety in Holland. I can still remember this great feeling of relief at having left the Nazi regime behind me. We had all heard – Jew or non-Jew, child or adult – of concentration camps and how sometimes an urn containing ashes would be delivered to a family.

It was still a long journey through Holland. I grew very tired but nevertheless managed to write a postcard to my other grandmother who lived in Karlsruhe with her daughter, son-in-law and my cousin. My father and I had been to visit them over the past Christmas 1938. We wanted to say goodbye to them because we hoped to be leaving Germany during 1939. Although she had another daughter in the USA, due to the aforementioned immigration policy my grandmother never got out of Germany and spent the war there until she was arrested and sent to the French concentration camp of Gurs. My aunt, although married to an Aryan, was also arrested and made to work moving heavy machinery. My cousin, as a half-Jew, was also in danger. He was hidden deep in the country by his non-Jewish relatives. Luckily the whole family survived the war and finally made it to the USA.

I dimly remember arriving at the Hook of Holland and getting on board ship. I was put in a small cabin for two. I went to bed immediately and fell asleep at once. When I woke up next morning the boat had already docked in Harwich. I was therefore able to write my postcard to my parents and tell them proudly that I had not been seasick. However, my companion in the cabin told me that while I was asleep the previous evening a waiter had come round all the cabins to bring us tea. I was upset to have missed this. We had some sort of breakfast before we got off the ship.

The indoctrination of fear over the past years and the apprehension of anyone in uniform, whether S.S. or customs official, was remarkable. We had been distinctly told not to go to the waiting train until the customs officer had put a chalk cross to indicate that our luggage had been passed. As soon as I entered the customs hall, a porter came up to me to take my suitcase to the train. I was terrified: what would happen to me without a chalk mark on my case? I desperately tried to indicate in sign language to him that I needed a chalk mark. I don't know how I made him understand; however, he smiled and took it to the customs man, who also smiled as he made his chalk sign on my case. This was strange behaviour indeed. I safely got on the train on the last leg of my journey. The train, I remember, belonged to the L.N.E.R. We were on our way to London – Liverpool Street.

My parents had been told that at Liverpool Street station we would be taken to a nearby gymnasium. In German *Gymnasium* means High or Grammar School and they were very impressed. They advised my Uncle Joszi to collect me from there. How disappointed they would have been if they had realised it was only a *Turnhalle* where one did P.E. Actually this gymnasium was the place where the children were farmed out to foster parents – Jewish or non-Jewish. Other children were taken on to Dovercourt, another assembly centre, where they were to stay for some time until homes were found for them.

However, there were about a dozen of us who were to be collected by relatives or friends and we were taken to another place. Years later I came upon it unexpectedly; a small synagogue building in a corner of Soho Square. Slowly, one by one, the children were met and taken away by their friends, until there were only two of us left. Eventually, the other child was also met by a relation. I remember this gentleman very well, because he stayed with me some time, to reassure me that my aunt and uncle would be along very shortly. But I was not the least bit worried. I was quite prepared to wait. It is amazing what frightens a child and what leaves him calm. I was scared about crossing the border from Germany and having any money – even only a few coppers – found on me. I was worried about being found not to have a chalk mark on my case in Harwich. But saying goodbye to my parents was quite casual. The mere thought that there was a possibility that I might never see my parents again never occurred to me. And now in a strange city, among people I did not know, why should I have qualms about my uncle collecting me ?

And of course I was right. Very soon after, both my aunt and uncle, totally out of breath, rushed through the door to greet me. They had, of course, been given the Soho Square address. But having had notice of the Liverpool Street 'Gymnasium' from my parents, they naturally assumed the meeting place had been changed. It all ended well. My complete faith in them had been justified. They brought me home to Amhurst Park. And I saw this strange city, where everyone drove on the wrong side of the road, where one could not know in which direction the buses were going because they had their destination on the back as well as on the front.

We got to Amhurst Park; it was a small house, not an apartment building. It nevertheless contained many people. I was given lunch and dinner and I had a special delicacy which I had never had before: tinned pineapple cubes, which I enjoyed very much.

I went to bed and fell asleep almost immediately. But all the excitement had perhaps been too much for me. In the middle of the night I woke up and was violently sick all over my bed. I have never liked pineapple since.

4

LA VIE BOHEME

There is a lot of difference between London and Berlin. There certainly was in 1939 for a little Jewish boy who did not know one word of English. I was to come into a completely different atmosphere and meet strange new people.

So there I was in north London, living in Amhurst Park, in an oldish house, which had certainly seen better days, in a road which had trolley buses going along it. These had only been in service a few years and were to remain one of the sights of London for another twenty-odd years. They were driven by electricity from the cables strung along overhead and were more flexible than the trams they were aiming to replace – but not very much. They were not stuck like trams in the iron rails, but could in some degree move from side to side, thus being able to overtake cars and horse traffic from time to time. But of course they could not overtake one another. When this was necessary it involved a major manoeuvre, with both trolley buses having to stop, the bus to be overtaken to have its guiders released from the overhead cable, so that the other bus could safely pass along the overhead cable. In the 1960s, with increased traffic and adjustments to traffic routes, these trolley buses became a liability and were phased out just as the trams were being phased out when I arrived in London. What astonished me at that time, though, was that once the

28

trams were withdrawn, the iron tram lines were left on the roads. They were just tarred over. In Berlin trams had also slowly been withdrawn, but the iron tram lines were immediately lifted from the road, as well as iron railings surrounding buildings, because, as everyone knew, iron was useful for Hitler's various preparations for war. As everyone in Germany – even I, an eight- or nine-year-old – knew that, why did no-one abroad realise it? Or did the Governments not really care? Of course, once the war started Britain also needed more iron and steel and the same thing was then done in London and other British cities.

The house where my uncle lived was also strange to me. Most of the houses in London were strange. In Berlin there were mostly apartment buildings where many families would live. Here there were small houses with sloping roofs in which only a few people lived, sometimes only a single family.

But however strange all this may have seemed to me, strangest of all were the people who were living in it.

It was a Victorian house in what must have once been a fashionable district, which had housed an affluent family with their servants. I don't know when it stopped being a one-family house, but by the time I arrived it had started its journey on the downward slope.

My uncle Joszi had been an actor in Germany, which was not the most useful career in an English-speaking country. His acting had, therefore, to be put aside for the time being. Later in the war he was to resume it successfully by broadcasting on the BBC World Service to Germany and making anti-Nazi films. It still amazes me – though no-one commented on it at the time – that in every wartime film the Nazis always looked extremely Jewish. In the summer of 1939, however, no such films were being made. Indeed work of any kind was very difficult to obtain. There were several million unemployed.

All his life he had avoided speaking English in case it would destroy his pure German accent on the stage. However, he had sufficient knowledge of English to be able to converse easily. When, therefore, this unemployed Englishman turned to the Jewish Board of Guardians for assistance, he was assigned two other Englishmen in a similar position, with the additional handicap despite their British passports of having not one word of English between them. My uncle was given financial assistance and told to look after them. They were provided with accommodation, first in a house bordering on Hampstead Heath, which later became the home of Michael Foot, the former Labour Party leader. Subsequently, they were moved to 96 Amhurst Park. And it was there that I met them.

They were given the basement flat. 'Flat' is a slight misnomer. It was, of course, not a self-contained flat, but two rooms below ground-floor level. There was also a kitchen and a toilet which was shared by other lodgers in the house. The kitchen did lead out to a beautiful garden, which was a wonderful attraction for me. I had only known tiny communal front gardens, paved back yards and local little parks in Berlin. By the time I arrived the brothers Weiss (that was the surname of the two gentlemen) had been joined by their old mother, who was an invalid confined to a wheelchair. The three of them lived in the front room, whereas my aunt and uncle had the back room onto the garden. My Aunt Hanna was not Jewish and therefore had no need to leave Germany. Very courageously she married my uncle during the Nazi period – when many other Aryan wives divorced the Jewish husbands they had married previously. She gave up her career and followed her husband into exile.

This was our living as well as our sleeping quarters. It was also Uncle Joszi's shop, but more about that later.

The ground floor was mostly occupied by the 'Persian Synagogue'. These were two large rooms, one to the front where all the men prayed at the weekend. The room at the back was for the ladies, who were of course not allowed to participate, but could listen to the proceedings from a safe distance. One could get to the garden from this room via a

30

huge, magnificent, Victorian glass conservatory built on stilts, with a heavy iron staircase leading down into the open. Although it was empty, without a single plant in it, I spent many happy hours in this wonderful glass palace. There was another tiny room on this ground floor, also occupied by a refugee lady and gentleman, whether married or not I never knew – probably not. They were also part of my uncle's charges.

The house was owned by a somewhat wealthy Persian Jew, who let these people live there at a reasonable rent. On the first floor there lived a Persian Jewish family who, for a reduction in the rent I believe, had to look after the Synagogue rooms during the week. The husband was much older than the wife. She was not yet thirty and had already produced three children, the oldest of whom was only a year or two younger than I.

At the very top, under the roof, were two attic rooms with extremely steeply sloping walls. The side of the room sloped almost to the floor. The upright wall space was no more than two feet in height. As yet these rooms were unoccupied. One of these rooms was destined to be the quarters for my parents and me.

It was an odd mixture of people as I was to find out in the next few weeks. The Brothers Weiss were the first Viennese I had come across. In the first weeks, as well as acquiring some English from this cosmopolitan crew, I also learned many Viennese expressions which in some cases varied greatly from the German I was used to. It is not only the USA and the UK which are divided by a common language.

The older brother Weiss, 'Ernstl', was by now, I seem to remember, working as a waiter or more probably in the kitchen of some restaurant. The younger brother, 'Fritzl', was at home, because the mother needed full-time attendance, including visits to the toilet. Fritzl, therefore, did all their housework and cooking. As the kitchen was shared by them with my aunt and the couple on the ground floor, this made for heavy traffic there on

31

occasions, not to mention intense discussions of how much gas had been consumed by each family.

Ernst and Fritz were visited by their girlfriends on their afternoons off, when the whole family and friends, weather permitting, would gather in the garden for a *Jause* – that is, afternoon coffee and home-made cake. The two girl-friends, 'Cilly' and 'Franzi' were working as domestics in nearby rich Jewish homes on Woodberry Down. These magnificent houses were torn down after the war to make way for a housing estate. But to my young eyes they were marvellous mansions with huge gardens leading down to an artificial lake, which was the local reservoir. I did get to see those houses once or twice, when we went to fetch unwanted furniture; this included iron bedsteads for my parents which were no longer required in these rich establishments.

The two brothers could not marry their girlfriends because they were married already. Being British passport holders they were, of course, much sought after by Jewish women trying to escape from the Nazis; as the wives of Britons, they automatically became British too and could freely enter this country. I now know that in the thirties W.H. Auden went through a form of marriage with Erika Mann, daughter of Thomas Mann, to enable her to leave Germany. The brothers Weiss also wanted to help some of their compatriots – at a price! I don't know what cash sums were involved. Now they each had to wait a number of years to obtain a divorce. When they were free to do so they did marry these two women friends. I believe there were also some other shady dealings; in any case there always seemed to be a certain tension between them and my uncle.

I cannot remember anything special about the couple on the ground floor living in what was then called 'sin'. Of course, the Synagogue only functioned on Friday night and Saturday. I did spend a lot of time with Family Yousopouff, resident on the first floor. They had two boys, Sami and Shimon, with whom I could play and who could also teach me some English; after all they had been here a few years already. There was also a little baby sister, Rebecca. The mother was a very kind-hearted lady. The family had travelled all over Europe trying to find a haven. My mother, when at last she arrived here, always admired Mrs Yousopouff, who had been in this country a couple of years, for her command of the English language. She used to listen to her in rapture when Mrs Yousopouff countless times told my mother her life story.

'I bin come from de Germanee mit tree children mitout anee monee . . . '

Mrs Yousopouff often used to invite me upstairs for their Friday evening meal. They were great rice eaters. They had several sacks of rice stored in their rooms. Every Friday afternoon I used to watch her as she spread some rice from the hessian sacks onto the table and carefully picked out various little black specks. It was only later in life that I realised that mice had got into the sacks of rice. It was their droppings she was removing.

They also employed a Persian Jew, a Hebrew teacher from their circle of acquaintances, who came to teach the boys. Naturally, I was also admitted to these lessons. Thus this became the most fervently religious period of my life. There was nothing my aunt and uncle could do to stop me facing east and devoutly praying at the oddest moments of the day or night.

Sami was always a good boy and hardly ever did anything wrong. Shimon was a lovable little rascal who always got into trouble, even when it was not his own fault. It was at those times that I learnt my Persian, for his mother always told him off in that language. I was told on no account to repeat these words as they were rather unsuitable to use in public.

A lot of time during those first weeks was spent looking after Uncle Joszi's 'shop'. The basement room had its innumerable uses. In addition to it being our bed- as well as our sitting-room, it was also the stock room.

Uncle Joszi had to make a living in some way. What he did was to go from house to house in the more prosperous parts of the district and offer the housewives there bars of soap, shoelaces, boot polish, handkerchiefs and other such small articles, which he carried in a heavy suitcase. He used to go to the East End from time to time, to the Hounsditch Warehouse, to replenish his stock. This stock was kept on shelves in our room. It was my task to tidy up the stock each day and when some neighbour came, who knew about our trade, to sell them one or two items and collect the pennies or twopences that these articles cost. It was hard work for my uncle and presumably not very remunerative. Later on he did manage to obtain a job as a machine presser in Simpson's trouser factory in Stoke Newington. This had to earn our keep: my aunt and uncle and myself and, when my parents finally arrived, their keep as well. As foreigners they were not allowed to accept paid work of any kind.

Uncle Joszi kept this up until the BBC broadcasts to Germany started. When his broadcasts became fairly regular he gave up trouser pressing. In any case, at that time one broadcast fee was more than the weekly pay packet at Simpsons. He remained with the German Service of the BBC more or less continuously for many years. In fact, he was still participating in a regular programme there when he died at the age of 78. The BBC broadcast a tribute to him the week after he died.

So money was tight all this time. We walked a lot to save the penny fare, but we never went far afield anyway. There was so much new all around me. The only time I really went any further was a trip to Windsor. My uncle had made friends with the local Jewish grocer in Seven Sisters Road, Mr Carr and his wife. He had persuaded them to give a guarantee for my parents. It was understood that my uncle would look after my parents and the Carrs would not be expected to help them financially. It was nevertheless a great responsibility they were taking on, because the Government would have held them liable should we have reneged on our promise to fend for ourselves. Their action saved my parents' lives. When the Carrs heard I was coming over before my parents, they offered to take my aunt and uncle and me in their motor car to Windsor Castle one Sunday. I had a lovely time going through the palace and sent a picture postcard to my parents. How I managed to thank the Carrs without knowing much English I cannot imagine.

The other great joy during those weeks was the garden. I had never known back gardens. Before coming to London I had always thought about ways of preventing Uncle Joszi from having to carry such a heavy case around the town. I thought of a different way of earning a living. I had therefore imagined that there would be a large front garden which we could utilise. We would entice passers-by to come in and try their luck with various games of skill that we would provide for them. I was sure we would be able to make a better and easier way of living. After realising that the garden was at the back, not at the front of the house, and that there were not many passers-by anyway, I had to abandon this idea. I had to be satisfied with selling shoelaces to neighbours. I could however indulge my enthusiasm for doing gardening, an enthusiasm I seem to have lost in later life.

In retrospect summers of long ago always seem to have been brilliant. But I believe the summer of 1939 really was a good one. In any case, I spent a lot of the time in the open. It was quite a long garden with a lattice fence towards the end. Behind this there was still a space which at a later stage I was able to turn into an open-air theatre. We also had a cat roaming around which my uncle named 'Johnny'. This turned out to be a misnomer when Johnny started producing kittens.

The end of the garden bordered onto the grounds of the church around the corner in Seven Sisters Road. The local Scout group met in the church and they often had their evening meetings in the open, sitting around camp fires singing their camp fire songs. I used to watch them shyly until one evening they invited me to join them. I rather reluctantly agreed, but as I did not understand what they were doing or what they were saying, I became rather frightened. So I left them and thought it was better to watch from a safe distance.

Among all the other uses of our basement room – bedroom, sitting room, dining room, stock room – it was also the library. My aunt and uncle had as many books as they were able to bring with them from Germany. Even at ten I had been brought up on Schiller, Goethe and Heine. I had read some of the poetry and some of the plays. I loved plays particularly and had found one which I read. It was *Reigen* by Arthur Schnitzler, which was later made into a famous film *La Ronde*. However, my aunt took it away from me because she said I would find it boring. I tended to agree with her. In every scene couples seemed to end up in bed even though they were not tired.

I not only read plays but I wrote them as well. Coming upon one recently I found it rather frightening that a ten-year-old could write a play called *Ohne Hoffnung* (Without Hope). It was all about immigration and the great difficulties of obtaining entry permits to other countries. It had, of course, a happy ending because a ten-year-old – in spite of all experiences – still believes that right will always triumph in the end.

I also wrote regularly to my parents. I still have a few copies of the letters that my parents kept. Here again, though of course in their way they are childish, I am astonished by a certain maturity in the concerns about daily life.

But all in all it was a very happy time, a very great contrast to my experiences in Germany. I went to the cinema for the first time in years. Jews had not been allowed to visit cinemas or theatres in Germany for some time. I enjoyed the novelty, even though I found it difficult to follow the plot. We never went to the cinema on Saturday night. That was when the box office put their prices up and it became too expensive. They charged one whole shilling (5p.)! There was even no school to go to – I was supposed to have started but the summer holidays intervened.

Finally, late in August, 1939, I was reunited with my parents, who had eventually obtained their permits to come to England in transit, while waiting for their visas to the USA. So everything seemed perfect. But it wasn't to last.

(See Appendix for Letters.)

5

PILLAR TO POST

My grandfather died in Berlin on 17th July, 1939, and my parents arrived in London on 18th August. Although I had been very happy with my aunt and uncle, I nevertheless missed my parents very much. To a ten-year-old two months is a very long time and I was ecstatically happy to be reunited with them.

I started school around the corner almost immediately. This was quite a difficult experience. Young children learn quickly and I had picked up a number of English words, but my knowledge of the language was minute. I can't remember how I reacted to the lessons. I am sure I understood very little. The teacher was very kind to me. But something I saw caused me great concern and frightened me enormously. What I saw was the cane and what frightened me was when it was used on the outstretched hand of some miscreant. The other boys seemed to take it quite calmly, but I had never seen a cane used before. Despite all the brutality that was about to happen, indeed despite all the brutality that had already happened in recent years, corporal punishment in schools was not permitted in Germany.

However, all this was not to last long. Within two weeks all children were told to assemble at the school on a Friday morning for evacuation. The impending war was looming ever nearer and it was thought wise by the government to get all the children out of large cities in order to avoid the anticipated aerial bombardment. This was the 1st of September, the day Hitler decided to invade Poland. We had our little suitcases and I was on my travels once again. I had travelled all the way from Germany just over two months ago. I had been separated from my parents all this time and had been reunited with them only two weeks ago. Now I was to leave them again. Indeed I left not only them but my aunt and uncle as well and also family Yousopouff, who lived in our house in Amhurst Park. The two boys, who were near my age, had become my friends through that summer. However, their sister, Rebecca, was only a baby, too little to travel by herself. So Mrs Yousopouff with her three children were evacuated together but unfortunately not on our train. Once again I was utterly alone, not really knowing anyone and this time not being able to converse in a language that I knew.

I really believe as a ten-year-old I had been very brave in the past few months with all the changes that had occurred. But now I was really lonely. Despite trying to be brave I was desperately unhappy. From Stamford Hill we took the train to Enfield. There we had to change trains and some hours later we arrived in the country.

We were taken to the village hall and our places were allocated. I was handed to an old lady who took me to her house. I am sure she was very friendly and welcoming but I had no idea what she was talking about. Something in me snapped and I started to cry. I ran back to the village hall, having hurriedly worked out what I would say to them.

As I saw the adults there, I cried out, 'I don't understand nobody, nobody don't understand me!'

My own teacher was still there. He took pity on me. He was there with his wife and son, who was a year or two younger than I. The teacher said I could stay with them at their place of evacuation.

We arrived at a big house and were shown into a room which had to accommodate all four of us. This was nothing new to me. In recent months I had got used to crowded sleeping quarters. What did surprise me however were the number of people in the house. I soon found out that most of them were servants. There was a cook, several maids, some men who were footmen or butlers or gardeners. Though I could not understand what they were saying, I got to know these servants rather well. The head of the household did not think that I or the teacher's son were suitable companions for him in his dining room. Therefore, the two of us took our meals with the servants in their quarters. They all treated us very well.

Although I was now with the teacher and his family, who were very kind to me, I still felt rather unhappy in these strange surroundings. The teacher's family tried to interest me in many things. They even succeeded in getting me to give them German lessons.

There were other visitors in the house. Amongst them was a lady who knew some German. She came to me on the Sunday. She told me that the Prime Minister, Neville Chamberlain, had just spoken on the radio. He had informed the nation that the country was now at war with Germany.

The week passed uneventfully. We went to school, came home to the servants' quarters. I said my Hebrew prayers every night. When the next Sunday came, the teacher's family were going to church, which was only across the road. They asked me whether I would come along or would prefer to stay at home. I really had no objection to going to church. So we all went across. At the entrance stood the owner of our house, welcoming everyone as they entered the church. From my time spent in synagogues in Berlin, I remembered that there the *Shammas* (the synagogue caretaker) would stand at the entrance and hand out prayer books. I naturally assumed that this gentleman welcoming us was some sort of church *Shammas*. It was only when he actually started to conduct the service that I realised he was a priest. In fact, he was addressed as 'Vicar' by everyone.

I had of course forwarded my new address to my parents, but the address 'The Vicarage, Yaxley, near Peterborough' had not meant anything to me until then.

In the local school I met two other refugee boys, brothers, whom I knew from Amhurst Park. They, being brothers, were of course boarded together. I now think that it was my influence that persuaded them to believe that they also were unhappy in their evacuation. In any case, we started to bombard our families with letters begging them to let us return to them. I remember the missives I wrote stating that no matter how humble the place we lived in at Amhurst Park and how magnificent the vicarage with its army of servants, I would never be happy in Yaxley. I asked them to come and collect me and signed myself 'Your Unhappy Herbert'. There is also a postcard still in existence where pressure was put upon me by the whole family (various aunts and uncles joined in) to stay put. But I was too determined for all of them.

After what seemed a very long time, but probably was only a few weeks, my uncle Joszi finally arrived to take me back to London. By this time, the war having started, my parents, as enemy aliens, were confined to London. They had to stay within its boundaries. So it was uncle Joszi to the rescue once again. I must however spare a word of gratitude to my teacher and his family whose names I am afraid I have forgotten. I must always be thankful to them for having taken me in with them and easing what would otherwise have been a much more fearful time for me.

Recently, my wife and I, driving on our way as guides at the Anne Frank Exhibition in Lincoln Cathedral, suddenly saw a signpost reading, 'Yaxley – 1 mile.' On our way back from Lincoln we made the detour to Yaxley. After fifty years numerous new buildings had appeared. However, the vicarage was still there with the church opposite, just as I remembered it.

Uncle Joszi and I returned to a very quiet London. This was the time of the so-called 'phoney' war, because nothing seemed to be happening. My mother understood it as 'funny' war and was very upset, because she could not see any humour in it.

My grandmother was still in Berlin. The outbreak of the war had destroyed any hope of her coming to England on a transit visa. Her only hope was now that her son Georg (Org), who had recently arrived in the USA from exile in China, would be able to bring her to the New World. However, the quota system over there would be against her.

My parents were still not allowed to work. Part of the time they spent perfecting their English. A refugee teacher had arranged classes on the premises of the New Synagogue, Egerton Road. There were many discussions amongst pupils and teachers about the mysteries of the English language – especially as spoken by Englishmen. One expression foxed them considerably. What was it the conductor on buses shouted once the bus started moving? (They still had conductors as well as drivers in those days). It was finally decided he called out 'Alright'. It took them a while to realise what he said was 'Hold tight'.

All the schools were closed when I returned to London. I did however go to the *Cheder* (religion school) in Egerton Road Synagogue. I also sang regularly in the choir there on Sabbath mornings. Finally, someone at the synagogue alerted the L.C.C. (London County Council) and persuaded them to start some sort of proper schooling on the synagogue premises. By this time a number of children in the area had returned to London. So my stop-start education started once more.

My parents and I and people like us were, of course, 'Enemy Aliens' now that Britain was at war with Germany. All adults had to appear before a tribunal. There were three categories of enemy aliens: A - B - C. C was the best category, known to be harmless and probably friendly. B were people one did not quite trust. A were definitely dangerous aliens. It was generally assumed that Jewish refugees who had to flee from Nazi oppression would be treated, even if as enemy aliens, at least as friendly ones. But so much depended on the chairmen of the tribunals, some of whom obviously had anti-German feelings and – dare I suggest it – some had anti-semitic ones. Indeed a number of refugees did get put into category C. My parents went to the tribunal. They were asked a lot of questions. My mother had to explain about her origins, how she was born in London, had been taken to Germany by her parents at an early age, had lost her British nationality by marrying a German.

The magistrate smiled at her and said 'And now you have come back to your country of birth!'

'Yes' she said.

A big 'B' was stamped on both their identification cards.

The war soon became neither phoney nor funny. Hitler started to eat up countries at a tremendous rate. Here in England, meanwhile, so many enemy aliens were running around endangering the country. All category A aliens and some in category B were soon rounded up, including my father. For some time we did not know where he was, until a pre-printed card, signed by him, informed us he was at least somewhere safe. But soon the war went even worse for the Allies and it was decided that all women in category B also had to be interned.

One morning two plainclothed policemen turned up at 96 Amhurst Park to arrest my mother. I was just recovering from an attack of mumps and was wearing a large scarf around my neck. The policemen told my mother she could take me along. They were quite kind and patient. They gave us plenty of time to gather a few belongings. Finally we left and were taken to the police station in St Ann's Road, Tottenham. There we saw a number of other women from the district in similar circumstances to ours, whom we had got to know over the past months.

The thing I most remember about the journey is the waiting. We waited many hours at the police station. Then we were taken to an assembly point in Fulham. There I was examined by a doctor. He threw my scarf on the floor and declared there was nothing wrong with me. We spent the first night there. Early next morning we were taken to Olympia station and put on a train. Hours later we arrived in Liverpool. They took us to a big hall – it was a boxing stadium, I believe – and we spent the rest of the day and the night there. We tried to get comfortable on the tip-up seats or lying on the floor between the rows of seats for a night's sleep.

The next day we got on a boat which crossed the Irish Sea. It was quite a rough journey. However, I was not seasick until the person next to me vomited. That just about finished me off! All this time we had no idea where we were going. Finally we arrived in Douglas, Isle of Man.

I shall never forget our reception in Douglas. As we came off the boat we saw a great crowd had gathered on shore. Doubtless they had read in the newspapers or heard on the radio about the dangerous enemy people who were about to descend on them. I have mentioned elsewhere that in Berlin I had a very long walk to and from school each day and frequently I was jeered and spat at when the German people realised I was Jewish. Now, as we passed crowds of people on either side, we were jeered and spat at not because we were Jewish but because we were German.

We were ordered to get onto the waiting train which took us to a place called Port Erin. This was a wonderful seaside resort with a long beach and many hotels along the front. The whole place had been taken over by the British Government for these women enemy aliens. I am sure the hotel owners were very grateful because the holiday business in this first summer of the war would not have been very profitable. We all got off and had to carry our heavy suitcases to the places to which we were assigned. Unfortunately, our destination was at the other end of town. We had to walk along the whole promenade with our luggage, which seemed to get heavier by the minute. This was not helped by some of our escorts shouting at us to hurry up. One lady in particular was rather vicious, though she could doubtless see that I – a ten-year-old – was struggling valiantly with my burden.

The place we came to was called 'Bradda Glen'. This was not an hotel but, I suppose, an early type of holiday camp. Once we got inside the main entrance there was a long narrow path with trees either side to struggle along until we came to what was to become the dining-hall. The site consisted of wooden barracks, bungalows and long dormitories, all of which was very pleasant in summer but rather damp and cold in winter. Fortunately, my mother and I did not stay that long but other people did freeze there the following winter. My mother and I were allocated a room in a building called 'Ladies' Hostel' (rather inappropriately for me). Once again we met a strange assortment of people.

The majority of internees were, like us, refugees from Nazi oppression. There were indeed a number of non-Jewish people, mostly servant girls, some of whom may have been Nazi sympathisers. But surprisingly there were quite a number of nuns. Most of these had been in convents for a long time. They had not come into contact with the outside world for many years. One in particular, I remember, enjoyed this brief interlude of unusual freedom. There were a number of children under sixteen who had to be educated. The school was near the station. Although I had been made to carry the heavy suitcase across town, it was felt that the twice daily walk to and from the school was too tiring for us. It was therefore decided we should have our own school on the premises, together with children from the neighbouring hotel. The teachers who taught us were mainly nuns. I still remember learning about the French revolution for the first time from one of them. Being taught by nuns was quite an education in itself. A nun's view of the French revolution puts quite a new slant on history. All this was in German, of course.

Via our relatives in London we at last heard where my father had ended up. He was also on the Isle of Man, but in the men's camp at Onchan. The number of letters we were allowed to write was greatly limited. My mother had to make use of my allowance as well. All letters were minutely examined by the censors. Only once was there a family meeting. All married men were allowed to visit their wives and children for a few hours. Some very determined unmarried men even managed to come to the women's camp in order to see their girlfriends.

45

At one point it was decided to send some of the interned men further on to Canada and to Australia. The ships sailed through U-Boat infested waters. One ship, the *Andorra Star*, was torpedoed and sank with many lives lost. When news of this reached Port Erin there was uproar. The women stormed towards the camp office and demanded to see the commandant. She finally came out and assured the assembled crowd that not one married man had been on board ship.

Immediately a cry went up, 'What about our sons?'

We were able to walk around Port Erin, although there were guards at the exit roads. However, there is not much to do in a place like that, especially if one is limited by money. We had to make our own entertainment. A number of artists and musicians were interned. For instance, three out of four of the future members of the Amadeus String Quartet met on the Isle of Man Internment Camp. In Port Erin there were a number of entertainment groups travelling round the various hotels. I organised a children's show at Bradda Glen. I also landed my first leading role in a short play called *Friedl's Dream*. I was, of course, Friedl.

Generally the war situation was getting worse. When at last the Nazis had overrun the whole of France and the German army had reached the Channel ports, many people became worried. It was then that one could begin to recognise the Nazi sympathisers; there were clear indications on their faces that they thought they would soon be liberated. Our own time for finally obtaining visas for entering the USA was approaching. A number of other people in Port Erin were in a similar position. However, we had to be able to attend at the American Consulate in London to receive the visas. The British Government decided to send this group back to the capital. So, once again, we were on our travels, in August, 1940.

Coming back to London did not mean we were set free. After all, these women and children were dangerous people. The place we were taken to under escort was in Wandsworth. As I mentioned earlier, all schools had been evacuated two days before war broke out and most of the pupils were still somewhere in the country, safely away from enemy bombing raids which, so far, had not occurred. One of these schools was the Royal Victoria Patriotic School for Girls, which had large premises in Wandsworth; these were now standing empty. The Government had requisitioned this building for these women internees.

The group assembled here was much smaller than in Port Erin, but so also was the area in which we could walk around. There were grounds surrounding the school. In fact after the war some council housing blocks were built there. At the time of writing the actual school building is used as a school for drama. At that time we were not allowed anywhere at the front of the building, although this was quite a distance from the main road. We could move around the gardens and yards at the back of the buildings. There was a smaller building which was given over to women with children. These were the typical dormitories with curtained-off cubicles for privacy. We stayed there only a few days because the German raids on London started almost as soon as we got back. The commandant of this London camp thought that in the circumstances it would be better for everyone to be under one roof. We took our mattresses and slept on the floor in the corridors, where there were no windows with glass which could shatter in any explosions.

The commandant, who had been one of the assistants on the Isle of Man, was a pleasant woman. She was a great improvement on the one on the Isle of Man. I remember she even joined in our weekly concerts, singing duets with one of the inmates. One of the internees waiting to get to the USA was Richard Wagner's grand-daughter. Surprisingly, unlike most of the rest of her family, she was anti-Nazi. She had a personal guarantee for her visa from Arturo Toscanini.

The situation in Wandsworth was completely different to that on the Isle of Man. The nightly air raids kept us awake for most of the time. But also we were much more restricted. We had no town to wander through and no shops to visit, as in Port Erin. When I needed a haircut I had to be escorted to a barber shop in the town. I enjoyed the few moments of freedom, being once again in the midst of bustle and traffic. A very small boy at the school desperately longed for a special toy, obtainable only at Woolworth. His mother asked me to get it for him while I was outside and to pretend to the escort that it was going to be a birthday present. The escort did indeed take me to the local Woolworth store to get the toy. But later she must have checked up on the little boy's date of birth. I got called by her and threatened with punishment for having induced her to take me to Woolworth on false pretences.

During this time some of us were taken in police vans to the American Consulate to obtain our visas. All our fingerprints were taken, just as they had been taken by the Nazis a couple of years earlier. At the Consulate we met up with my father. He had in the meantime been brought from the Isle of Man to Lingfield Race Course, where the internees were housed in the stables. Finally the day of our release came. A passage to America had been booked and we were allowed to await departure back in Amhurst Park. It is a long way from Wandsworth to Stoke Newington and as we drove along we saw the extent of the damage the bombs had done – bombs we had so far only heard.

At this time Britain stood alone against the Germans. The Nazis had conquered most of Europe. They had not yet invaded Russia, nor had the United States yet entered the war. Hitler could let loose his whole venom against this island, whose government had refused to prepare, or prepared too late for war. Britain stood alone for a whole year. It was only when in the summer of 1941 Hitler decided to turn east that some relief came to this country. The bombing of civilian targets was tremendous.

Hitler himself boasted '*Ich werde ihre Städte ausradieren*' – I will rub out their towns – like Coventry!

The nightly air raids and even daylight raids continued. It was no longer safe for my mother and me to sleep at the top of the house, under the roof. Luckily, family Weiss had moved out, so we took over their basement room. We were happy in the thought that we should soon be in the States. As the time for departure slowly drew near we were only waiting for my father to be released. He was still interned at Lingfield. The departure date arrived and went. My father was still interned. We missed our ship. By the time my father was released our visas had expired and had to be renewed. We booked another passage and had to get new visas. By this time, due to the constant air raids, the American Consulate had been evacuated to Epsom. The three of us went there for our visas. All these journeys were an enormous expense for us. We were being interviewed in Epsom when there was a knock at the door. A lady entered. After making sure we were indeed family Levy, she told us that our places on board ship were needed for essential war workers, who had to travel to the States. We would have to wait for the next ship. That was in January, 1941. The fierce Battle of the Atlantic was about to start. All passenger ships were withdrawn for many months. Our new visas ran out, so did our American guarantees. We were left in war-torn Britain, without money and without work.

6

WARTIME LONDON

Mr Neville Chamberlain once told Hitler he had missed the bus. The Levy family had literally missed the boat. After waiting years for the entry visa to the United States, we had at last obtained these precious documents only to be told that there was no way for us to get across the Atlantic.

We were stranded in wartime London, dependent on the earnings of Uncle Joszi, with whom we lived, to keep us fed and clothed. The air raids continued all through the winter of 1940/41. My Uncle Poldi's business premises were burned down during the Blitz when the City of London erupted in an inferno as great as the fire 300 years previously.

We soon realised that we all would have to vacate the premises at 96 Amhurst Park. My Aunt Charlotte, her husband Fred and their daughter Ellen-Eva had left North London some time ago and had moved to a flat in Hampstead. While my father was still interned and we were eagerly waiting for his return, my mother and I often used to spend weekends with my aunt's family in Belsize Square. We stayed there overnight. As the nightly air raids continued we all, including other tenants in the house, used to take our bedding down to the basement boiler room. It was safer to sleep there than in other parts of the building. I am not sure whether, as enemy aliens, we were actually allowed to stay away from our own homes. I have an idea that there was a curfew for us each evening, when we had to return to our residence. However, no-one seemed to worry about this. It wasn't too safe in Amhurst Park either, even though it was a basement room; the glass in the window had been shattered some time ago, when a bomb fell nearby. The glass was never replaced but treated canvas was put into the window frames; this smelled and also made the room even darker than before.

As time went on there were fewer and fewer windows with glass panes to be seen. Those that were still about had strips of tacky tape strung along them to prevent the shattered glass falling all over the place once it got broken. The shop window panes were never replaced; if they did break, they were boarded up with hardboard. Sometimes a tiny square of window glass was put in the centre, so that the goods could be displayed. There really was no longer very much to display. Every type of goods was getting to be in very short supply. Queues formed everywhere and everyone became queue joiners. Many people, not knowing what they were queuing for, joined queues on the off-chance that they might get something that could be of interest to them. I myself remember, later in the war, going with a group of friends to the Salad Bar of the Lyons Corner House in Coventry Street, near Piccadilly Circus. The great attraction was that one could eat as much as one could manage for 2/6d., (12½ pence). Naturally one had to queue to get in and so we joined the queue. There were only two of us boys among a number of girls. A lady came up and stood right in front of my friend.

Rather upset, he told the lady 'The end of the queue is back there'.

She turned on him and asked, 'Do you realise this is the queue for the ladies' toilet!'

Food was severely rationed. Butter was limited to a quarter pound per person per week or even less; some people divided their butter ration into tiny squares for each day of the week. Fruit was mostly unobtainable although children got an additional ration of oranges, when available. Bananas became a rarity. Indeed, there were children who had never seen one and did not know what to do with them when, after the war, they were imported once again. The Black Market became a big racket; some retailers kept goods 'under the counter'.

At this time people were going to Underground stations to spend the night on the platform. Later on, iron bunk-beds were provided and everyone had an assigned place. We did try it once at Manor House Station. We never got as far as the platform, as it was already overcrowded. We spent the night with many other people in the passageway leading to the booking office. It was not very safe, but it was better than nothing and there was no glass to shatter. We were there with my Aunt Ellen. She used to talk to everyone in her heavily German-accented way until someone asked her where she came from.

'From across the road,' she quickly replied.

I returned to Egerton Road Synagogue for services and also for school. I must have been a bit of a hero – after all, I had been in prison! I also learned something of a novel game called cricket, played at school in the concrete yard. Everyone had to retire after having scored a maximum of 10 runs. Egerton Road was not exempt from bombing raids. One bomb scored a direct hit on a house opposite the synagogue. It killed all inhabitants, including a fellow pupil of mine.

My education was haphazard. The school in Egerton Road was only a temporary wartime affair. I had missed the 11+ examination. Possibly I would never have passed it anyway because my English, although getting better, was by no means perfect. My Uncle Org had written from America not to worry. Things were different in the States. He would see to it when we got there. But we never did get there. I eventually attended my first proper school in a couple of years in Kilburn. Finally, I did sit for a scholarship. One of the tests was an essay, a word I had never come across before, though I knew all about English compositions. In spite of that, to my great surprise, I was awarded a scholarship. There was only one drawback. The only available schools not evacuated out of London were one for cooks and the St Martins School of Art. The headmaster of St Martins would have taken me, but advised my parents strongly against it. He thought my talents did not lie in that direction. There was a possibility to join a local grammar school, but here there was another drawback. At this time a weekly fee had to be paid. It was all of 5 shillings (25p.) and my parents really could not afford it. School leaving age at that time was 14. I stayed in the school in Kilburn until that age. The headmaster however advised my parents to let me continue schooling. He suggested the Clark's Grammar School at Cricklewood. I was transferred there and managed to matriculate. Even though my parents were earning a little better at that time, I do not know how they managed the school fees, which then were considerably more than 5 shillings a week.

London was dark at night. There were no street lights. All windows had to be covered fully with thick, preferably black, material so that no chink of light could escape. People used to walk around in the dark with tiny torches. Even so, some Air Raid Wardens complained about too much light; but the No. 8 batteries necessary for these torches were almost unobtainable, so that often the torches could not be used. There were few cars, as petrol was strictly rationed and only available to essential users. What few cars there were had their headlights covered, allowing only a narrow slit of light to escape. The inside of buses were lit with a minimum of light. Few people went out at night and tried to stay as close to home as possible. There was a poster campaign which asked 'Is your journey really necessary?'

Once my parents realised that we had to abandon our plans to go to America, they applied again for work permits. The situation had changed radically now. With so many men in the forces, extra hands were needed for specific tasks. My father received permission to do war work. He went to a timber factory which made wooden munition boxes. My mother also was able to work at home, weaving shopping baskets. As we had to leave our present accommodation and my parents had a steady, even if only a small income, they decided to look for a flat of their own. It had always been my mother's desire to move to Hampstead and be near her sister. At that time, flats anywhere were easily obtainable at quite low rentals because many people had left London for the safety of the countryside. Therefore, towards the end of 1941 we moved to Greencroft Gardens, off the Finchley Road.

While still living in Stamford Hill I had met, through my aunt Charlotte, someone from Hampstead. This was Karl-Heinz Guttmann, who at weekends often came to visit us. We had a large garden, with a whole separate section at the back. Here we had made an open-air theatre with a stage where we could put on shows. We also opened our own youth group, called 'Youth-Up', of which we were joint chairmen and, for most of its time, its only two members. When, therefore, we moved to Hampstead, I already knew someone there. My parents also joined the New Liberal Jewish Congregation (now the Belsize Square Synagogue) which had been started by refugees from the continent. Although the prayers were mainly in Hebrew, the sermon was always in German and was to remain so for many years. The first Rabbi was Dr. Salzberger, who was asked to initiate religious instruction for the young people. There were only three of them at the time – Karl-Heinz Guttmann, Norbert Cohn, and me. The lessons were held on a weekday afternoon after school. We all had to be home early to avoid the black-out.

Hampstead has always been in a class of its own. In 1941 it still retained something of its artistic aura. After all, it had been only a couple of years before that Benjamin Britten was living along the Finchley Road. There was no crawl of traffic then. Finchley Road was a tree-lined avenue with wide pavements. No traffic lights at Finchley Road Station or at Swiss Cottage. A friendly policeman half-heartedly controlled the intermittent traffic and happily went home in the evening. Instead of a huge Waitrose foodmarket, there was the welcoming John Barnes department store on three floors, with a small Woolworths squeezed into its middle. Harben Parade was still a row of dilapidated one-family houses, ready to be torn down once the war had ended. Refugee actors had opened their own little theatres there, like *The Blue Danube*. Around the corner in Eton Avenue was the *Laterndl* (The Lantern). There were no parked cars anywhere crowding the streets. As one went up the wide Fitzjohn's Avenue one passed the Everyman Cinema towards Whitestone Pond. Here on Sunday mornings there would be speakers of every political conviction. In the summer months artists would display their paintings. Going down again, to South End Green, one could still visit the bookshop on the corner, where George Orwell had worked for a time; now it is a pizza parlour. Hampstead was still an artists' quarter. Swiss Cottage became the focal point for Jewish refugees from Germany, so that some wags began calling it *Schweizer Häusl.* A lot of German was heard there during the war, though everyone was encouraged to speak even faulty English, rather than perfect German, on the streets. The New Liberal Jewish Congregation (Jews from Germany and Austria) had its premises in a flat in nearby Buckland Crescent.

We had a top floor small flat of three rooms, kitchen and bath. It was self-contained and for the first time in many years I had a room of my own. Most of the raids had stopped by the autumn of 1941 and we could safely stay on the top floor.

What was there to do at home, once you no longer had to go to the shelter? There was no TV. There had been limited transmissions for a few years until the war started. The majority of people had never seen television. They certainly did not own a set. We, as enemy aliens, were at first not even allowed to own a radio. Once we were given permission, there were no sets available. Through his work, one day my father managed to get hold of a bakelite set. The set had an open back and my father was able to make a wooden one at his factory. This radio opened a whole new world to us. We mainly listened to the news of course. We could even listen to it in German, which was broadcast on the World (then called European) Service. There we could also hear the features in which my Uncle Joszi and Aunt Gisa participated. After the war we heard from Gisa's sister Margot (who, unlike their mother, miraculously survived the war in Germany) that she and her non-Jewish husband had secretly listened to the broadcasts and she had recognised the voices of her sister and her cousin.

I discovered a whole lot more on the radio: the top shows at that time were *Itma*, with Tommy Handley, and *Hi Gang* with Bebe Daniels, Vic Oliver and Ben Lyon. Once the Americans joined the war they sent over recordings of their best radio shows with people such as Jack Benny and Bob Hope. And there was something called *Transatlantic Quiz* with participants from both sides of the Atlantic. There were classic serials and *Saturday Night Theatre*. There was *The Man in Black*. But best of all, there was *Children's Hour*. I learned to love Dickens from the first of the many weekly episodes of *Nicholas Nickleby*.

And there was the cinema. The theatres at that time were beyond our means.

During the first years of the war they opened at odd times. At the start of the war all theatres were closed for some time. Slowly they began to reopen. Some of them had only matinee performances. Donald Wolfit did a season of Shakespeare matinees. When they did eventually have evening performances, these started rather early at 6.30 or even 6. But the cinemas did their best business during the war. There really was no opposition. Long queues formed every night. Especially for the cheaper seats one might have to wait for hours. When one eventually got in, it might be in the middle of the main film, so that one knew the end before one had seen the beginning.

Later on when the war was going better for the Allies, in 1944, the great seasons of the Old Vic Company at the New (now Albery) Theatre began. At the time I did not realise I was witnessing one of the high points of British theatre history. What a wonderful group of actors: Ralph Richardson, Laurence Olivier, Sybil Thorndike, Margaret Leighton, Joyce Redman, Alec Guinness, Harry Andrews, the list is endless. And the wide range of plays: *Peer Gynt, Richard III, Henry IV* (both parts), *Cyrano de Bergerac, Oedipus, King Lear, St Joan, An Inspector Calls.* I saw all this from the gallery. There was an odd system; these seats were not bookable in advance, of course, but if one got up early, at about 6, one could queue there in the morning before school. At about 8 o'clock a lady sold 'queuing stools', i.e. a ticket would be issued for a numbered little wooden folding stool, which one could sit on in the evening until the gallery box office opened. Then it was a matter of quickly buying your ticket and rushing up the stairs to ensure you got one of the better seats. They were not individual seats, but benches. For a popular play the management squeezed you up as hard as they could. Uncle Joszi, who often came with me, likened the attendant to General Montgomery, as he instructed the movement along the benches in order to get one more person into the row. The earlier you got there in the morning for your queuing stool ticket, the better chance you had in the evening. While you were sitting on the little stool in the evening, you were entertained by buskers. They had strict rules in which order they could entertain us and then pass the hat round for our contributions.

At times one could almost forget about the war. One of the songs of the day was, 'You'll get used to it', but then slowly news began to trickle through about the horrific things that were happening on the continent. No-one could fully believe it at first and there are people who, despite the evidence, refuse to believe it still.

The tide was slowly turning. Hitler was being pushed back in Africa, in Italy and in Russia. I remember on my way to school hearing that the Allies had landed in Normandy on 6th June, 1944. Then the air raids began again and it was back to the shelter. This was Hitler's last throw. These were the 'revenge' weapons, *Vergeltungsmassnahme* 1 and 2. V.1s were the pilotless planes, or 'doodlebugs' as they popularly became known. They were aimed in the general direction of this island. Their range was irregular and their direction at best indiscriminate. One could hear them approaching quite clearly, because of the droning noise they made. While this noise was heard one was quite safe. Once the motor stopped, when the engine had cut out, one knew that an explosion was imminent and that the explosives might descend on one's own house. These things came over by day or by night.

One afternoon, after school, I was with my mother in Greencroft Gardens. The alert sounded. We heard a doodlebug approaching. We hurriedly went into the corridor to avoid any glass. Suddenly the droning stopped. It seemed almost overhead. There was a large explosion. The bomb had dropped two streets away in Broadhurst Gardens. We had escaped with nothing worse than shattered windows.

When people left for work in the morning they never knew what or who they would find in the evening. We spent most nights in a basement shelter along Finchley Road. Sleeping was rather difficult among so many people. Another friend of mine, Heinz Kuttner, was next to me. We used to laugh at the strange noises people made when they were asleep. Finally we had to be separated to stop us disturbing other people with our giggling. I often did not fall asleep until early in the morning and then my parents did not wake me in time to go to school. Lessons at school were often interrupted by the daylight raids and all pupils had to assemble in a windowless corridor. We could only return to our lessons once the All Clear sounded. One day on my way to school I saw a road was closed. I pleaded with the Air Raid Warden to let me through to my school. On my way past all the damage of the previous night I saw people, still in their nightwear, frantically searching.

V.2s were an early form of rocket. There was no warning, no-one could hear them until just before their impact, when they made a whistling noise. Luckily I never got so near to one as to hear that. But those were the last gasps of Hitlerism. Soon Germany was being squeezed on two fronts.

As the Russians from one side and the British and Americans from the other pushed the German army further into retreat, the whole horrendous picture of atrocities came into the glare of full publicity. The newsreels revealed the utter inhumanity of these people.

But Victory had to be celebrated. V.E. Day (Victory in Europe) was proclaimed on 8th May, 1945, my father's birthday. In the evening my cousin Ellen-Eva and I took the tube to Oxford Circus. We came out of the station to see huge crowds. All the streets were lit up for the first time in many years. As we walked down Regent Street I saw the bright yellow lights of the Austin Reed building in the distance. People were dancing and singing. Piccadilly Circus was one big street party.

They sang a song composed only a few months earlier 'I'm going to get lit up when the lights go up in London'. The lights of London had gone up. Everyone was looking forward to a happy future when there would be no more wars.

7

INTERNATIONAL LONDON

Britain is an island and certainly until the advent of the second world war the British were very insular. After all it was the Prime Minister, Neville Chamberlain himself who talked about Czechoslovakia as being a distant country about which we know very little. What were the British, and particularly what were the Londoners, to make of the fact that during the war London became an international city with so many foreigners?

Long before the US had entered the war and their troops were sent over here, when little boys went up to G.I.s and asked them 'Got a gum, chum?' or English adults referred to these US soldiers as, 'overpaid, oversexed and over here', there were plenty of other strangers on these shores. There were firstly the troops from Australia, Canada and other Commonwealth states. As Hitler invaded and overran so many European countries, many citizens, especially troops, from those places sought refuge over here in order to continue fighting the Nazis. So we had the Free French, Free Poles, Free Czechs, Free Dutch, Free Norwegians among many others. There was even a Free French Theatre, producing plays in that language. But in Hampstead there was *The Laterndl* and T*he Blue Danube Club* doing plays and revues in German .... German, in London, in the middle of the war!

Indeed there were many Free Germans, for a number of

them had fled from that country too and they had formed their own Free German League of Culture (*Freier Deutscher Kulturbund*). While they were mostly Jewish refugees from Germany, there were also a number of political refugees. All political parties other than the Nazi party had been banned in Germany years before. So any known Social Democrats or Communists, who had not been imprisoned, thought it wise to leave the country – illegally if necessary – and continue their fight against the Nazis from abroad.

The Communists had a difficult time of it for a number of reasons. Some had gone to the Soviet Union. When Stalin formed a friendship pact with Hitler in 1939, their position became precarious. While this pact lasted a number of these people were forcibly repatriated to Germany. Those in the Soviet Union who escaped that fate found, once the pact was broken two years later, that they were considered spies. Many disappeared without trace. Among these was a famous left-wing actress Carole Neher, who had appeared in the 1931 film version of *The Threepenny Opera*. Nevertheless, some survived even these tribulations. They were able to return and take up their positions in post-war East Germany to form a government. After the war those Communists who had fled to the West rather than to the East came under suspicion.

The Free German League of Culture in London found its home in Upper Park Road in Hampstead. It was an alliance of many factions, but gradually came to be dominated by members of the Communist group. At times German Communist attitudes towards the war became extremely difficult and uneasy; they had to tread most carefully. They were, of course, anti-Nazis, having barely escaped with their lives from Germany. But they were also adherents to the policies of the Soviet Union. Therefore, this contradiction of a Soviet-German friendship pact put them in a quandary. Their solution to this dilemma was to maintain that Britain's war against Germany was an imperial one, which they could not support, and that they had to bide their time. This they did and happily the situation was resolved within two years,

61

when the Soviet Union and Britain became allies.

The League put on many cultural activities as well as holding anti-Nazi meetings. They had their own small theatre where plays like Wedekind's *Frühlings Erwachen* (Spring Awakening) and J. B. Priestley's *Sie Kamen an Eine Stadt* (They Came to a City) were put on. They also wrote and performed topical revues among which the most successful was *Mr. Gulliver goes to School* . At their meetings and activities they had the support of prominent English people, including Sir Julian Huxley, Eleanor Rathbone and Michael Redgrave. Artists of international standing lectured and exhibited, including Oskar Kokoshka and John Heartfield.

I was a boy of 11 or 12 and knew little about the politics. I knew that my aunt Gisa – actually my mother's first cousin, Gisela Lietke, an actress – was a member and she asked me to come along to a special children's party. I went and when she asked whether any young person wanted to entertain us in any way, I immediately put up my hand. Rather reluctantly she called me up on to the stage and I did one of my recitations. She was agreeably surprised and in later years encouraged me to take it up professionally. The Free German League started up a children's group. There already was a youth group: *Freie Deutsche Jugend* (Free German Youth) but I was too young for that and had to make do with what became known as the Younger Youth Group – the Y.Y.G. The Free German Youth was known by its German initials: F.D.J.

The Younger Youth arranged an afternoon called *Werke Deutscher Meister* (Works of German Masters). The date happened to be 30th January, 1943 – ten years to the day since the Nazis came to power. We had poetry by Goethe, Schiller and Heine, music by Schubert, Mozart and Haydn. This was all in German, but slowly and steadily in our age group English began to take over. We used to meet every Saturday afternoon. We printed our own newspaper. On summer Sundays we went on rambles. On occasion we spent the enormous fare of 6d.(2½p) on a 102 bus to go to

Epping Forest. We held an art exhibition of work by refugee children, opened by Lady Clark, wife of the then Sir Kenneth Clark (later to become Lord Clark, author of *Civilisation*). The exhibition was attended by Jan Masaryk, Foreign Secretary of the Czechoslovak government in exile. There is still a photo of me next to him, looking at the pictures. Jan Masaryk returned to Czechoslovakia after the war, but jumped from a balcony (or was he pushed?) after the 1948 Communist takeover. I stayed with the Younger Youth Group for most of the war and spent many happy Saturday afternoons there. It all finished when the war ended.

I was also able to join the more adult FDJ, mostly for their theatrical productions. I took part in one of Lessing's one-act plays *Die Juden*. All this was in German. My cousin Ellen-Eva, through our aunt Gisa, had joined the FDJ sometime ago and was a member of their choir. The FDJ had been founded by someone called 'Appel' Buchholz. This nickname had been given him not solely for his round and rosy face, but because he had been named Adolf by his parents. At this time he was not particularly happy at this choice of name.

Appel had an interesting history. As a non-Jew he had nothing to fear from the Nazis on that account, but as an active member of the Communist Party of course he had. His life was in danger in Germany and he therefore managed to escape to Czechoslovakia, before that country was overrun. Once the Nazis invaded he had to get out quickly. He somehow made his way to England, on the way picking up a group of Jewish refugee children. He found homes for all of them in this country and he also made friends with the Wrightson family.

I only met him once during his stay in England, though I saw him several times after the war. It was sometime during 1944 that my cousin Ellen-Eva and I went to Quix Green, near Reading, to spend a few days with the Wrightson family. The Wrightsons had three daughters of their own. They had also taken in a Jewish refugee boy from Germany called Heiner. By this time Heiner had forgotten most of his German in this English environment and was to forget it altogether by the time the war ended. Although his mother had been killed in a concentration camp, Heiner's father survived the war and he managed to trace his son. The two met and were unable to converse with one another. During these years of separation, Heiner had become estranged from his father; he felt much more at ease in the English atmosphere in which he had grown up during the war. It was mutually decided that the Wrightsons would adopt Heiner formally. Heiner however kept up contact with his father who emigrated to the USA.

All this was in the future when Ellen-Eva and I arrived in Quix Green. We were very hospitably received by the Wrightsons. I still remember the marvellous record player they had on which I was able to listen to *Peter and the Wolf* – all on several 78s records; no CDs then, or even Long Playing records. Appel was one of their guests. Numerous other visitors turned up each day including a number of American airmen from a nearby aerodrome. I was to hear later that one of these young men, who had been particularly jolly and amusing, had been shot down on one of the raids over Germany shortly afterwards.

The three of us – Appel, Ellen-Eva and I – came back together on the train to London. What I did not know, but was to hear later, was that all this time Appel had been trying to play a rather more active part in the war against Hitler. The British did not want to use him. He succeeded with the Americans. He trained with their Air Force and agreed to be parachuted behind German lines to reach friendly contacts. One day in 1944/45 he was put into an American plane and once they were over Germany he jumped at a pre-arranged spot. At this time the Germans were retreating both in the West and in the East. Appel was dropped far to the East, dressed as a German with full German identification papers. The only trouble was that where he landed had by that time already been conquered by the Russians.

The house in Berlin in which Herbert Levy lived. His parents and grandparents had adjoining apartments on the first floor, both with balconies.

Salomon and Bianca Levy, Herbert's grandparents.

Phillip and Jettchen Stein, Herbert Levy's grandparents.

The four Levy children: Selma, Paul, Irma and Arthur (Herbert's father).

The five Stein children in 1912. Back row: Leopold (Uncle Poldi), Joseph (Uncle Joszi), Rose (Herbert's mother). Sitting: George (Uncle Org), Charlotte (Auntie Lotti).

Phillip Stein,
Herbert Levy's grandfather.

Rose Stein and Arthur Levy – engagement photograph.

Herbert Levy and his cousin Ellen Eva in Berlin. This photo was exhibited in Berlin with the caption 'Two Beautiful Aryan Children'.

Herbert Levy,
two years old.

Herbert Levy's class
outing at his Jewish
school 1937/8. Most
children in the photo
did not survive the war.

Joseph Stein (Uncle Joszi) as The President in Schiller's drama *Kabale und Liebe* (Intrigue and Love).

Johanna Storbeck/Stein (Aunt Hanna) as Michaela in Bizet's *Carmen.*

Herbert Levy leaving Berlin by *Kindertransport*, June 1939.

The garden in Amhurst Park, N.16. (The church where the scouts met is in the background.) Back row: Fritz Weiss, Uncle Joszi, Aunt Hanna. Front row: Shimon Yousopouff, Mrs. Weiss.

The garden in Amhurst Park, N16. Herbert Levy with his aunt and uncle and a couple living in the house.

Children's concert party in Port Erin internment camp, Isle of Man 1940. (Herbert Levy first on left).

Herbert Levy in 1945.

Lilian Levy on her wedding day.

Herbert Levy during National Service in Beverley, Yorkshire.

Herbert Levy with his family – son Andrew, daughter Hilary, son-in-law Mike, wife Lilian.

It was quite difficult to explain to the Russians that this German was in reality a member of their allied American forces. He managed nevertheless to convince them, but his life must have been in the greatest danger until he succeeded in doing so. The war soon ended with the complete defeat of the German forces. Appel now wanted to return to England to marry my cousin. However, Britain would not allow him to re-enter this country. The reason given was that he had left England during the war without obtaining an exit visa. It would have been impossible to do so, as he left on a secret mission about which no-one could be told.

Was this the real reason, or was it an excuse because he was known to have left-wing leanings and to be a member of the Communist Party? As soon as the war was successfully completed, tensions arose between East and West, which were to last for many years. Nevertheless, for the rest of his life he always retained an affection for Britain. It had given him refuge during the war. But permission to re-enter was always refused. My cousin Ellen-Eva therefore packed her bags soon after the end of the war, went to Berlin and married him there.

At times she, too, had difficulties in getting back to this country, although she had left these shores quite openly. Her mother, my aunt Charlotte, was very ill a few years later and she desperately wanted to see her daughter again and also meet her two grandchildren, Sylvia and Fred, who had been born meanwhile. I spent several days at the Home Office trying to arrange entry permits for them. The Home Office seemed to have a full file on the family and knew all about their political affiliations. The authorities eventually relented and Ellen-Eva and her two children came on a visit to their mother and grandmother. However, Appel never saw England again.

8

'BLISS WAS IT IN THAT DAWN TO BE ALIVE'

It is difficult now, for anyone who was not there at the time, to imagine what the 1945 election and its aftermath were like. I was not quite 16 and not yet even a British citizen, so I was unable to vote in any case. But the whole episode, even in retrospect, was an exciting time to live through.

The signs were not auspicious. A great war had been won and the acknowledged architect of that victory, the flamboyant Winston Churchill, was the leader of the Conservative Party. Next to him Clement Attlee, the leader of the Labour Party, seemed insignificant. When someone told Churchill that Attlee was a modest man, Churchill replied that he had a lot to be modest about. Churchill had stood firm against the Nazi threat and he had become the symbol of the fight for freedom against dictatorship, so the nation had much for which to be thankful.

Yet the country was tired after a protracted war, which had not yet been fully won. The menace of Japan had still to be defeated. But in Europe the war was over and there was a deep desire everywhere for a new start and a better life in the future than that of the immediate past in the inter-war years. Churchill was too much associated with the war. The polling industry was in its infancy and no one paid much attention to their findings. Churchill seemed to take it for granted that a grateful public would entrust him with the administration of his country in peace time. Moreover he misjudged his public during the election campaign.

There was no television at that time, so that the campaign was mainly concentrated on public meetings and in election broadcasts on the radio or wireless, as it was then called. Churchill was a well-tested and competent broadcaster, who had inspired the nation with his wartime speeches. But now he overplayed his hand. In the most notorious broadcast he compared the men of the Labour Party, who had been his colleagues in the wartime coalition cabinet, to the Gestapo. This was said a few months after the death camps had been liberated! It was to cost him dear.

In another election broadcast, Churchill compared the Conservative way of success to a ladder, which each one had a chance to climb and reach the top. Even as a teenager I realised that there was room for only one at the top of the ladder and in order to reach that position one would have to push down any number of people on the way – much like Disraeli's 'greasy pole' in politics. The public in general seemed to have similar feelings. In the public's mind Churchill was associated with war and the people wanted peace. On the morning of the election *The Daily Mirror* in one of its most effective headlines had a picture of a revolver with Attlee and Churchill on either side, with the caption 'Whose Finger on the Trigger?' The desire for a complete peace as quickly as possible was paramount.

There was a landslide victory for the Labour Party. Not only did they have an overall majority for the first time, but a huge superiority of numbers. The actual scale of the victory seemed to surprise everyone. The most unlikely seats fell to Labour. The good wishes of many people went with hopes for Labour success – and much was expected of them. For the first time a Labour Government could put their plans into practice without having to look over their shoulder because they needed the support of minor parties.

In fact a great many things were achieved. Despite shortages, fuel crises, an exhausted public and a nation near bankruptcy because of the war, Attlee and his cabinet were determined to achieve their vision of a new and more just

Britain. The Welfare State, now frowned upon, was inaugurated. It is difficult nowadays for younger people to imagine what life was like before the war and what changes occurred in those five or six years of a Labour Government with a large majority. The nationalisation of the public utilities and the coal mines; the expanding of the education system, so that for the first time, apart from a few scholarship boys, higher education was available even to people who were not wealthy; the arrangement of proper pensions and the gradual elimination of poverty and unemployment. Perhaps the greatest achievement was the setting up of the National Health Service. The pre-war situation is very well described in A. J. Cronin's novel *The Citadel*. Now no longer was there a Lady Almoner in the hospitals with whom patients had to bargain how much they could afford to pay for their treatment. No-one had to worry whether they could afford the medicines on their prescriptions. People could go to the dentist without fear of what it would cost them. Cheap spectacles on the counters of Woolworth disappeared because everyone could go to an optician to have his eyes tested and clinically examined so that a correct prescription could be given. The number of people needing proper glasses was so great that the optical industry was overwhelmed. In the first year or so it took several months to have the spectacles made up, so huge was the demand.

The Conservative Party voted against a Health Service. But not only that, they also used every means of publicity to frighten people. During the war there had been someone called The Radio Doctor who spoke on various programmes giving advice about the common cold and similar ailments on the BBC. His voice was recognised throughout the country. The doctor in question turned out to be Dr. Charles Hill, who in later years became a cabinet minister in a Conservative Government. Now he appeared on newsreels in the cinema – there was no full television service as yet – railing against what he called 'socialist medicine' when no doctor would be free to treat his patients in the way he wanted. Changes were put through continually. Although there were shortages due to the ravages of war, it was a time of hope looking forward to a brighter future. It was a time when it was thought that things had changed for ever and that the bad old days of poverty, unemployment and down-and-outs on the streets would never return. There were still people alive who could remember the Victorian age, who knew that it had not been a Golden Era but an age of crime and poverty. Now it was a time when most people thought of the common good rather than of their own advantage. During those five years a revolution had taken place without a single shot having been fired.

Alas, it could not last. The Welfare State was slowly dismantled – not immediately but almost unnoticeably. Like Wordsworth's, it proved to be a false dawn. Yet it was exciting to be young then and to live through those changes and experience tells me there always is another dawn.

9

AN ACTOR'S LIFE FOR ME

My uncle Joszi was an actor, his wife Hanna was an opera singer, his cousin (my aunt) Gisa was an actress, so I suppose that acting was in my blood. I cannot remember a time without at least reading or listening to plays. Even in Germany, when I was quite a little boy, I recall sitting around the table with my parents, grandparents and other adults, listening to Uncle Joszi reading from Schiller's *Wilhelm Tell*. At one point he had to stop the reading, as I had burst into tears. I had been totally overcome by the wicked Gessler's demand that Tell with his bow and arrow should shoot the apple from his son's head. I had to be pacified and assured that all would be well in the end.

I learnt poetry and used to recite at birthday parties. My grandfather was always very proud of that. Although I was not supposed to hear it, he frequently whispered to my grandmother how much better I did it than any of the other children.

I never did take up acting full-time, although my aunt Gisa, before she returned to Germany after the war, had a long talk with me to encourage me to take it up professionally. But I had known so many actors and knew what a hard struggle it is all one's life. Nevertheless, I can never forget the thrill of stepping onto a professional stage, of hearing the orchestra strike up and the swish of the curtain as it is raised, to have the glare of the stage lights on you and to sense the expectation of the audience out there. I have been short-sighted since I was about 13 years old, so I could never really see the audience. Nowadays one would wear contact lenses. One year, when I did a summer season at Sadler's Wells Theatre with the old D'Oyly Carte Company, I played an executioner's assistant in *Yeoman of the Guard*. For this I had to wear a black mask. I was able to wear my glasses underneath the mask. A whole new world opened up, as I could see the reaction of individual members of the audience in the first few rows.

While I was interned with my mother on the Isle of Man during the war I did my whole repertoire of German poetry and got into the plays that the children put on there. When we were interned in London at Wandsworth I wrote my own poems to recite at the weekly performances. If there was nothing suitable to put on at my open air theatre I wrote my own plays. I wrote a play about the Nazi period when I was only 10. When I was 13 I wrote a play called *Pardon My Impersonation* to be performed with my friends in the youth group to which I belonged.

This group met during the war on the premises of the Free German League of Culture at Upper Park Road. I was very much at home there. I attended many of the plays that were put on by professional actors. In that way I met a lot of them, many of whom were later to play all the Nazi parts in British wartime films. My uncle at this time was working in the German-language propaganda broadcasts at the BBC. Whenever they needed a child's voice, they asked my uncle to bring me along. At the BBC I met a number of actors who were to become known on the British screen, such as Herbert Lom and Albert Lieven. The man in charge of the German Service at that time was Walter Rilla, who had been a well-known film actor in Germany. His son, Wolf(gang), later directed a number of British films. The Service was subsequently run by Marius Goring, the classical actor; he was English, but his German was remarkably good. He was married to the German actress Lucie Mannheim; she is probably best known to English audiences as the mysterious stranger in Alfred Hitchchock's version of *The Thirty-nine Steps*. Shortly after the war the two of them toured Germany with a two-hander called *Third Person*. One night they would play to Allied troops in English, the next they would do the play in German for a native audience. For a time Lucie Mannheim and my uncle appeared on the BBC German Service in a series about a Berlin working-class married couple.

I took part in a number of broadcasts over the years. I remember going to various BBC studios. There is the Maida Vale studio in Delaware Road, which is mainly used for music. It was also occasionally booked by the German propaganda service. I actually had to sing on that occasion. It was *Frère Jacques* and I had to give of my best, as I was supposed to be a young French child suffering under Nazi occupation, nevertheless speaking in fluent German to my tormentors!

During the war the BBC had requisitioned the old Criterion Theatre in Piccadilly Circus as a studio. This theatre was built below ground level and was thus far safer from daylight air attacks.

At that time recordings were not yet made on tape but on discs only. Before any recording, the announcer would speak into the microphone to say 'Disc room calling, disc room calling; we shall start recording at . . .' One could not cut out any fluffs, but the whole disc had to be destroyed and the passage re-recorded. One had to be much more careful and much more accurate the first time. The microphones were considerably larger than today and much more temperamental. They had to be treated with respect. One of the actors there was the Austrian, Martin Miller. It was he who started up the Austrian refugee theatre *Laterndl* in Eton Avenue. He was a very excitable actor, who fully lived every part. He would always get too close to the microphone, so that the director put a chair in front of it in order to keep him at a distance from it. Another actor, one of tremendous size and weight, Gerhard Kempinski, tried silently on tiptoe to pull Martin Miller back by his jacket tail while other members of the cast tried to suppress their laughter – all to no avail. As he reached the climax of his scene, Martin Miller simply reached for the chair, picked it up and threw it aside. Another wasted disc.

Bush House in the Aldwych was, and still is, the headquarters of the World (then European) Service with many studios. It was well guarded during the war. No-one was let into the building without permission. One gave one's name to the security guard, who phoned through to the studio. Once the producer had given his permission, one got a chitty which had to be presented and signed by the producer, to be shown to the security guard on leaving the building. On one occasion I omitted to get a signature from my producer, was unable to find him when I noticed this and then spent a long time till I finally made my exit surreptitiously via the basement. I think it would have been easier to explain my predicament to the security guard. I still have the unsigned voucher as a memento.

The main broadcasting studios of the BBC are in Broadcasting House in Portland Place – a huge building and a perfect maze. The German Service sometimes booked a studio there. I remember one broadcast dealing with Schiller's *Ode to Joy*. This is now well known not only because Beethoven used it in the *Choral Symphony*, but because that part of the Symphony has been adopted as a sort of National Anthem of the European Community. It was however on that occasion that I first learned that Schiller, instead of calling the poem *An die Freude* (Joy) had meant to call it, *An die Freiheit* (Freedom). He had to abandon this however, as it was thought by his publishers to be too revolutionary. In 1989, when the Berlin Wall came down and Leonard Bernstein conducted this symphony in the open air there, he restored the original title and the chorus sang about Freedom and Joy.

After the war I attended drama school at Toynbee Hall in the East End of London. That put me in touch with Sadler's Wells (now English National Opera) where I spent about 15 years doing non-singing roles. Apart from the marvellous experience, it was also a great thrill to be at close range when, English opera and English singers were emerging from the war. I met and heard so many great singers. Among these was the Belfast tenor, James Johnston, who was just a little ahead of his time. This was before jet-set singers, otherwise he would have had an international career. I was also there for the debut of Amy Shuard, a wonderful soprano. Both of them later sang at Covent Garden. So also did that great bass, Howell Glynne.

I participated in over a hundred performances of *Die Fledermaus* and I suppose must be able to recognise each note in it. Other operas I learned to enjoy through my participation were *Faust, Schwanda The Bagpiper, Eugene Onegin* and *Fidelio*.

One great and really unusual event was that I appeared in the first ever professional production in England of Verdi's *Simon Boccanegra* – to appear in the premiere of a Verdi opera, even though it was some 40 years after the composer had died! It has since entered the regular repertoire over here. But the first production in 1948 was a great success and is still referred to as a landmark. It was an exciting evening, with the most wonderful music. There is a tremendous duet in the prologue between baritone and bass (Arnold Matters and Howell Glynne). There is a stirring trio in Act Three between baritone, soprano and tenor (Matters, Joyce Gartside and James Johnston). But the high point of the evening was always the council chamber scene at the end of Act Two and the whole Sadler's Wells Company did it proud. Somewhere there are still some 78 r.p.m. recordings of this scene.

Once I met Vaughan-Williams, who was a frequent visitor to the theatre. He came for a rehearsal of *Hugh The Drover* and gave us instructions on how to dance as Morris Dancers.

Odd things always seem to happen on the stage at Sadler's Wells. I was not on stage in *Carmen* when the tenor accidentally swallowed his stuck-on moustache, nor when in the same opera the tenor, bending to pick up the flower

Carmen had thrown to him, split his trousers. However I do remember one occasion in the council chamber scene in *Simon Boccanegra,* where I had a very quick cross from one side of the stage to the other while drawing out my heavy sword, I found I had the handle in my hand without the blade.

The stage at Sadler's Wells is relatively small. The scene changes in *Schwanda The Bagpiper* on a dark open stage with raised curtain were a nightmare. In *Fledermaus,* in the party scene in Act Two the stage was crowded and had to be cleared for the ballet interlude. In one of the performances one of the girls in the corps de ballet twirled too near the long table full of champagne glasses and brought all the glasses crashing down. Another time, one of the girls lost her tutu and quickly had to rush off stage. *Fledermaus* was always one of the favourite operas of the chorus. They could demand more glasses of champagne from the footmen. There actually was no champagne but only cider.

Perhaps the most exciting time was back in 1943 when I was 14 and did a film test. The actress Tatiana Lieven was at that time married to Miles Malleson, who was a well-known screen and stage character actor. He had also written a number of screenplays and had translated Molière. He appeared in his own version of *The Miser* at the Old Vic very successfully. At that time a film version of Louis Golding's *Mr Emmanuel* was being prepared. The two of them recommended me to the agent Rita Cave as suitable for the part of a young refugee boy. She therefore arranged for me to have a film test at Denham Studios. At that time Denham was the biggest and most luxurious film studio in England, which had only been built a few years previously by Alexander Korda after his success with the Henry VIII film.

I had to go there several times, which was quite exciting in itself. At this time I hardly got out of London; it being the war, we could not go on holiday, nor could we really have afforded it. The first time I had to go to Irene Howard, the sister of Leslie Howard who had recently been killed when his plane had been shot down over the Atlantic. She was the casting director and gave me my test scene which I had to learn. I remember the huge corridors which led to the various studios. There were different coloured lines along the wall to lead you to the correct one. Denham Studio was very busy at that time with a number of films being made. In the open there was a set representing part of a large ship. Later on I realised this was the setting for a scene of the wartime film *The Way Ahead* then being made by Carol Reed, who later became very famous with *The Third Man*. Laurence Olivier was also very busy at the studio at this time, with his first Shakespeare film *Henry V*. I saw many of the extras dressed in their armour coming into the canteen for their lunch break. When Rita Cave came with me, which she did for the actual test, we did not eat in the canteen but in the refectory where all the stars met. Among the actors I saw there was Googie Withers.

One of the people testing that day was a little girl called Jean Simmons from Golders Green. She was to play the daughter in the house where Bruno, the refugee boy, had found shelter. Her mother, Mrs Cooper, was played by the actress Elspeth March, who was the wife of Stewart Granger. How odd that both mother and daughter were at one time or another married to him. The actor who played Mr Emmanuel was Felix Aylmer, who was later knighted. He played many character parts in pre- and post-war films, but this was his only leading part and he gave a fine performance. Although my scene was with Mr Emmanuel, I did not do it with Felix Aylmer. The scene I had to do was after the boy Bruno had been rescued from the sea where he had been trying to swim to his mother, who was still in Germany. He was recovering in bed and Mr Emmanuel came to see him. Bruno had to explain to Mr Emmanuel what he had been doing. The setting, the bed with a part of the wall behind, the lighting, the camera had all been put up. The director, whose name was Harold French, would read the part of Mr Emmanuel for the test. He told me to get into the bed. Of course, I only had to take off my shirt and put on a pyjama top. That was all that would be seen of me. Everything else was covered by the blanket. We rehearsed the scene once; at one point he told me to turn my face towards the camera, which was quite close to me. I could see my reflection in the glass, which was a little disconcerting. Then we did the scene properly with camera rolling. I hoped I had done well. But there were weeks of waiting. Finally I was informed I had won the part. I was tremendously excited. But there was a drawback. As a foreigner I needed a permit to work. Sadly it was refused.

Tatiana and Miles Malleson wanted me to have another go, to audition for an American play about a Nazi boy called *Tomorrow the World*, to be produced in the West End, but I was too disappointed with my film test experience. I have always consoled myself that very few child actors make it into the adult world. Jean Simmons is one of the rare exceptions.

10

IN BUSINESS

Wartime education was rather haphazard. Many schools were evacuated, others had closed down. Lessons were often interrupted due to air raids or discontinued altogether because the building had been bombed. The effect was seen at the end of the war when it was discovered (as I did when I joined the Education Corps) that 2% of wartime children were illiterate. Even those who had more or less received continual education obtained little learning. The vast majority went to Elementary schools (as opposed to Grammar schools) where the school leaving age was 14. These young people left school without any educational certificates nor any skills or qualifications whatsoever to go into the working world. There they would become navvies or factory hands or possibly office boys, if their handwriting was good enough. There were a number of young people who, because of wartime conditions, had failed to be filtered through the 11+ net or were late developers. Thus they were doomed to remain in these dead-end jobs. I remember one young man in my class (a brilliant scholar) who would have been condemned to this life. However through some lucky chance he managed to get an interview at the Post Office. He was offered a place as a telegraph boy, which he was told could lead to better things if he applied himself.

It was therefore fortunate for me that at this stage my

parents were able to transfer me to a fee-paying Grammar school, where I could matriculate a few years later. But even then university places were at a premium. Most of the modern universities did not yet exist. A very small fraction of the population went to the relatively few places available either by being able to afford to pay or being able to obtain one of the handful of scholarships. I was not too concerned as I was still hoping to enter the theatre. That was not to be.

Meanwhile I had to go out and earn a living. I therefore had to find a job in the world of commerce.

I applied and got a position with The Standard Trading Co. Ltd., a wonderfully all-embracing name which did not give away too much about its activities. The company actually dealt in sausage casings or skins, which is apparently a very specialised trade. At that time there were already experiments with artificial or plastic skins. However, the bulk of business, well over 90%, was done with natural skins – that is the intestines of various animals, mainly hogs and cattle.

The Standard Trading Company, despite its grandiose and confidence-inspiring name, was really a one man business. I was its only employee apart from the owner. However, it shared offices with another company in the same trade who had a shorthand typist. This staff of two was shared between the two firms. I worked for the Standard Trading Co. in the mornings and changed over with the typist in the afternoon. The owners of both businesses (there were two of them in the other firm) had come to this arrangement in order to share expenses and also to share information from the mail that arrived every morning.

The offices were in the City Road near Old Street Station and were very Dickensian. Our rooms were on the top floor of this office building, which had an elevator-well around a central staircase, protected with iron railings. There was the old-fashioned metal lift, which went up and down for everyone to stare at, travelling at an amazingly slow rate. It involved a somewhat protracted time to reach the fifth floor from ground level. It was serviced by a young man, probably no older than I, who was the son of the caretaker for the whole building. The young man seemed to have a lot of trouble in making the lift stop at the right level of each floor, which meant many jolts up and down near floor level before the lift doors could be opened. When this young man was at lunch, the lift was unavailable, so one had to walk up or down or both.

The offices consisted of three smallish rooms – one for the director of the Standard Trading Company and one for the two directors of the other firm. The third was for the staff of the two firms. There was no central heating but open coal fires. This was the winter of the fuel crisis so that often no coal was obtainable and one's fingers froze. Thus any writing or typing was done with great difficulty.

I had been engaged because of my knowledge of German and French. As my director of the Standard Trading Company was Polish, my tasks included correcting his faulty English as well as German. I don't think I was capable of correcting his French! My introduction into the world of commerce was an eye-opener and confirmed my pre-conceived fears of the capitalist world.

The arrangement was for the two companies to share any information in the mail. This seemed to work satisfactorily for the first few weeks that I was there. However, things soon began to change. There was a lot of mail for each firm every day, coming from all over the world. There were many letters from Shanghai, which was still an international commercial city at that time. The Communist takeover was still some years away. Most of the business was done by mail. There were no fax machines and few telexes. The international phone service was in its infancy – certainly there was no direct dialling abroad. Even calls outside London had to be connected via the operator. Information, orders and offers had to be sent quickly. Often airmail letters were too slow so the details had to be despatched by telegraph. This sometimes involved quite lengthy messages which were sent in code, not in order to keep any secrets but in order to hold costs down. One code word would encompass long phrases. There were huge volumes of established code books, where one could encode one's messages and the recipient could then decipher them with his own copy of the code book. I remember one such book was the long-established *Rudolph Mosse Code*.

The discussions between the rival owners decreased gradually. The connecting door between the two offices stayed closed longer and longer and finally was locked. One day a second desk arrived in the office of the director of the Standard Trading Company. I was told that I should do my morning stint in his office and not take out any correspondence. I noticed when he wanted to speak to me he called me up to his desk or came close to mine. Suddenly he started to whisper and put his hand in front of his mouth, so that I complained I could hardly hear him. He indicated that he did not want the people next door to hear. This farce also went on in the afternoon with the typist. The two owners of the firm next door did not seem to notice or, if they did, did not comment on it.

It was an international business where goods were bought mostly from China, India and South America and resold to the European continent. All shipments were made by sea. The consignments were sent off with mind boggling initials, either C.I.F. or F.O.B., sometimes even C. & F. These curious letters of the alphabet turned out to mean, 'Cost, Insurance, Freight' or 'Free on Board' and sometimes only 'Cost & Freight'. It was soon after the war when, due to the shortages worldwide, anything sold easily. Otherwise I do not understand how they could have conducted their business. They did not carry any stock, nor did they improve or alter the goods they bought and resold. The Standard Trading Co. did not even buy anything before it was sold. They would obtain or solicit offers from, say, Shanghai and re-offer the goods to a single importer in Switzerland. This Swiss importer would issue an Irrevocable Letter of Credit for the sum involved. My firm in turn would on receipt of this issue a Letter of Credit for a smaller sum and pocket the difference. For all I knew the same procedure happened in Switzerland.

To my young and socialistically inclined mind these seemed very strange proceedings, confirming all my prejudices of capitalist mendacity. Moreover, strict instructions were given that the goods, which were packed in wooden casks, were to have no identifications except the special marks and numbers by which they were identified on the Bills of Lading. Once these Bills of Lading came to us, one of my tasks was to ensure that the name of the exporter was cut out before the Bills of Lading were forwarded to our clients. This seemed to me to be the typical abuse by the middleman, who did nothing to improve or alter the goods but simply acted as a postman: a completely unnecessary function and much like the anecdote that is told of the consignment of sardines that had been travelling around the world for many months. It was sent from continent to continent, consigned from trader to trader. At last one trader decided to check up whether the sardines were still fit for human consumption. When he opened one tin, an indignant sardine turned on him and shouted 'Hey, mister, we're not here to be eaten, we're here to be bought and sold!'

We never even saw the goods as they were mostly destined for the continent and never came anywhere near these shores. Many of the consignments went to Tangier, which at that time was an international city. Tangier had a wonderful trade smuggling goods into Spain. At one point we were inundated with orders from Tangier. I am convinced that most of our goods to Tangier were destined for that trade, though we of course were not involved in smuggling.

Very rarely the goods were intended for the UK . They would then arrive at the London Docks, which at that time were still in full swing. London was one of the busiest ports in the world. Once my director took me with him to the Docks to have a look at these sausage casings that I had heard and written about so often, but had never seen. We took a taxi to the East End. It was most difficult to get into the docks as there were long queues of huge lorries waiting either to collect their goods or to deliver new consignments.

Finally we arrived at the correct warehouse, found the right casks and got some of the dockers to undo the lid of one of them. These intestines were heavily salted to preserve them in good condition on the long journey from Shanghai. All the skins had to have certificates that they had been inspected, had come from healthy animals and were fit for human consumption. My director took out one of the skins, which were of various lengths. To show me he opened it up and blew into it. The dockers around him watched with great interest as the white intestine inflated.

They gaped in amazement as they saw what was happening until one of them exclaimed 'Cor, they're fucking French letters!'

There was great amusement and laughter all round. My Polish director looked up smiling. Not knowing the euphemism 'French letters' he doubtless thought they approved of the way he was able almost effortlessly to blow up the intestines. On the other hand he might have wondered how these dockers knew about the improvements I made to his French correspondence.

I stuck it with the Standard Trading Company for more than three years. When I finally left it was to serve my term of National Service in the Army. There I also came across a whole new assortment of strange and peculiar people, previously completely unknown to me. But that is quite another story.

11

GONE FOR A SOLDIER

At the end of the war in 1945 all the troops were demob-happy. They could not wait to get home to their families. But Britain at that time still had numerous commitments all over the world. Apart from the occupation forces in Germany and Austria, there were many places, especially east of Suez, that required guarding. As the newly independent nations that had been part of the British Empire were slowly emerging after the war, there were a number of trouble spots and revolutionary insurgents in places as far apart as Malaya and Kenya. The regular army was not large enough to cope with all of this. Thus, for the first time, National Service in peace-time was introduced in this country. All 18-year-olds had to serve in one of the three arms of the forces, at first for two years and later for only 18 months.

When, shortly before my 18th birthday, notices went up about my age group having to register, I went to the local office. At this time my parents and I had not yet received British citizenship. I was therefore sent away again and told I would be called when wanted. Within two years I was in the army.

A great number of Jewish refugees, including many younger people, had applied for naturalisation after the war. People below the age of majority, which was 21 at that time, had become British through their parents. The

84

government had to decide on a cut-off point beyond which these young men would no longer be called up. This important deadline was two months before my date of birth, so I might have missed all of this if I had been born two months earlier.

Sometime before the end of 1949 I received a notice that I had to report to Bromyard Avenue in Acton for a medical. I passed this and was interviewed by an officer, who told me my application to join the Educational Corps would be considered. I heard nothing for about four months and secretly hoped that they had forgotten all about me. But well into 1950 I received a notice that I was to report to Winchester on a certain day in April, as a candidate for the Royal Army Educational Corps.

My thoughts during the journey from Waterloo to Winchester were in turmoil.

I did not know what to expect. I was really completely ignorant about the army and about army life. My mind must have been full of apprehension, yet the only thing I remember of that journey is looking out of the train window and, as we neared our destination, I saw the recurring sign, 'You are entering Strong Country'. Strong was the least of what I was feeling right then. I later learned that Strong was a particular brand of ale.

A number of us gathered on the platform at Winchester and a corporal bundled us into a lorry, which took us to a camp outside Winchester called Bushfield. This had recently been vacated by the Americans, who had used it during the war. It was now a training camp for the K.R.R.C. These were the initials of the King's Royal Rifle Corps, apparently a crack regiment which had its Headquarters at the barracks in Winchester itself.

There were a number of us who had opted for the Educational Corps, but for the most part these were young men who were to spend their period of service in the infantry. All of us had to stay in Bushfield for our ten weeks of basic training after which those of us who were in the Educational Corps would be transferred to the Army School of Education for further training. We were given basic equipment and uniform and training would start in the morning.

The K.R.R.C. at this time had amalgamated with the Rifle Brigade of Balaclava fame. Apparently this was one of the most desirable regiments in which to serve. Entry of officers was restricted only to those who had attended either Eton or Winchester. Some who had served in the regiment in the First World War included future Foreign Secretaries and Prime Ministers. At the time I got there the officers doing their national service included sons of toothpaste and toothbrush millionaires, owners of famous racecourses and also the son of a Foreign Secretary. The actual private soldiers included people from the roughest parts of the East End of London. During my ten weeks at Bushfield I met all kinds of people from either end of the spectrum whom I had never met before and whom I really knew nothing about.

We had been there only one day, when we were already divided into the 'better class of person' and the 'worse kind'. The officer material was sought out and set before something called WOSBee, which stood for War Office Selection Board. This council of officers decided who could be removed from the common flock and put into O.C.T.U. – the Officer Cadet Training Unit. The army is full of such initials and to someone like myself, who knew nothing about the army, it was confusing. One Grammar School boy was terribly incensed at his rejection at W.O.S.B. due, he thought, to the fact that he had not been to a Public School. I assume he could have made it even so – but of course never to one of the elite regiments; the R.A.S.C. (Royal Army Service Corps) might have been his destination. The O.C.T.U. candidates were immediately taken away to another part of the camp and did their training far away from the common herd. The Educational Corps candidates, possibly because they would have further training later, were left with the 'underclass'.

The army sets out to break one's spirit and to make sure that any spark of individuality withers as soon as possible. It is maintained that this is necessary for orders to be obeyed without question in wartime. They therefore give you the most menial tasks they can think up. One gets a uniform that preferably does not fit. One gets a tremendous number of webbing, including belt, braces, anklets, buckles and pouches, which has to be scrubbed and painted a particular colour with blanco. One is given two pairs of boots of a dull black colour, which have to be made to shine with spit and polish. All the materials for this (blanco, boot polish, etc.) have to be paid out of the weekly wage which, at that time, was 28/-(£1.40). One has to fold one's sheets and blankets each morning and lay out all one's kit on one's bed in a special way for kit inspection. People go along with pieces of string to ensure that all the items on the ten or twelve beds on each side of the barrack are in the identical place on each bed. All this to ensure that one stops being an individual. An extraordinary amount of authority is given even to the lowest lance-corporal. Full use is made of this authority, not to say that often this power is abused. I vowed that if ever I were in such a position, as I would be unless I was R.T.U.'d (Returned To Unit), I would try not to abuse my position.

We had our usual amount of square-bashing – being marched up and down the parade ground. We had weapon instructions, like taking Bren guns to pieces. This being the late spring, we spent a lot of time in the open, quite an unusual occurrence for me, so that my arms and face took on a new colour. I was interviewed and asked what games I played. When I mentioned tennis, I was told that was not suitable for a rifleman. The Educational Corps recruits were treated with even more contempt than the ordinary privates. I suppose this was because those in charge knew that after ten weeks we would be out of their jurisdiction.

When some of us, at one weekend off, went to see the Salisbury Arts Theatre Company, who were visiting Winchester, in a performance of T.S. Eliot's *Family Reunion*, this was frowned upon. We were getting above ourselves.

They were the longest ten weeks I can remember. It

consisted of bullying and petty chicanery. When one weekend we were given a 48-hour pass, we were kept waiting for inspection at the guardroom, in order to make quite sure we would miss the London train. At one point it got so bad and the queue so long, that the R.S.M. (the Regimental Sergeant Major) came along and let the whole crowd of us leave en masse, without any further inspection.

Here I also learned, really for the first time, of the endemic antisemitism that exists both in the 'lower' as well as in the 'upper' classes. It was never something open or violent, except on the occasions when someone felt openly aggrieved about a situation. However there was often a slight reference to money – either about one's vast quantities of it or of a certain tightness in wanting to spend it. Sometimes there were passing references to physical characteristics. At this time there were still Church Parades on Sunday mornings. Everyone, no matter what his religion, was taken to Winchester and paraded on the square. Soldiers were dismissed to attend the churches of their particular denomination. Jews did not have to attend a church. However, no soldier was allowed to be found walking along the streets during the time of the church services. This made it rather difficult for me. On one occasion I went with a fellow soldier to a Methodist service. At another time I met a co-religionist by the name of Mendelssohn and we went to have morning coffee in the lounge of an hotel. However, on a weekly pay of 28 shillings I could not do that too often.

I suppose with time there developed a certain camaraderie as we were all fellow sufferers. And then there also developed – which no doubt was the aim in the first place – a desire to act as a team, to do well, to ensure that one's troop or one's company did better than the rival group. It was ten long weeks. The only diversions were journeys away from Bushfield like my trip to Aldershot to be fitted for the official army spectacles. When these were broken due to some strenuous battle training, I got another day off to go to Aldershot to have them repaired. It was on this occasion, on my way back, that I saluted the cook. We had to salute all officers and were told when in doubt salute. Without my glasses it was difficult to tell the difference.

This was barely five years after the end of the war. We were all informed that we were training for the next war and we were left in no doubt that it would be the Soviet Union who would be the enemy. At this time the period of National Service had been reduced to 18 months. Shortly after joining up, the war in Korea started and everything was to change. I vividly remember discussing this event with a friend I had made in the camp. It was clear to both of us that South Korea had invaded the North. We both agreed that within a short time it would be put about that it had happened the other way round and that history would be persuaded that this indeed was what had occurred. Time has proved us right.

I made a number of friends. There was a great variety of characters: farm boys, city types, barrow boys. I suppose a certain bonhomie crept in as we got to know each other better. There were the passing-out parades, followed by passing-out parties, where passing out were the operative words. The new riflemen were posted to their battalions, which at that time were in Germany. The Educational Corps recruits had to go to the Army School of Education.

At that time the School of Education was in the process of being moved from Bodmin to Beaconsfield in Buckinghamshire. Most of it was still in Cornwall but one or two units had already moved to the Home Counties. It was a toss up where we were to go. We did not know until almost the last day that orders had come for us to go to Bodmin.

There were about thirty of us and, as we were thought to be intelligent, trustworthy beings, it was believed unnecessary for us to be escorted by any officer or N.C.O. This was some years before the Beeching massacre of the British railway system and we were all set for a very long but very comfortable and enjoyable train journey. There were several train changes. One of them was in Oakhampton, I remember. It was indeed a great relief from army barracks, loud commands, absurd drill. It was a very civilised way of travelling and a pleasant way of spending a day in good company with interesting conversations.

We finally arrived at Bodmin station late in the evening. There was no-one to meet us. So we enquired as to the whereabouts of the camp and with our heavy packs and equipment slowly made our way up the hill. We gave them all a great surprise. No-one was expecting us. It soon became clear that we had been sent to the wrong place and frantic telephone calls were made asking what was to be done with us. I am quite sure there had been equally frantic phone calls earlier in the day from Beaconsfield when we had failed to turn up there. Thirty trustworthy and intelligent young men had gone A.W.O.L. (Absent Without Leave) en masse. I am sure everyone was relieved that it was only one of the Army's usual cock-ups.

This was the beginning of the weekend and nothing could be done with us until Monday morning. Meanwhile we had to be kept busy. So we were told to spend the weekend changing the colour of all our webbing to the one prevalent in that area. I was pretty sure it would be a useless exercise as I thought it likely that we might have to change it to a third colour once we got to Beaconsfield. This proved to be perfectly true.

In any case we had another day's pleasant journey across the south of England. We travelled via London this time. We arrived at Paddington and had to make our way to Marylebone Station, where the train took us to Beaconsfield. The contrast between Beaconsfield and Bushfield is hard to imagine. There would have been a difference in any case even in Bodmin but a number of additional unusual factors made it even more marked. Beaconsfield camp had only just been opened. We were only the second group to be there. Together we made up a company of about seventy people. The other half of this number had done their ten-week training with a Welsh regiment in Brecon. They had been sent to the correct place first time round. The camp was in the middle of the most attractive Wilton Park. Also we had a most unusual C.O.

This company commander, a major in the Black Watch, had recently become the Major Lord Wavell. His father, who had just died, was the famous wartime Field Marshal Wavell who had fought with such distinction in the Middle East, Greece and Asia. He had also been Viceroy of India. Both father and son had received injuries in wartime – the father had lost one eye, the son an arm. Both were men of culture. The father had published a book, *Other Men's Flowers*, a selection of his favourite poetry, apart from other books on war and strategy. His son was one of the most unusual officers I met during my time in the army. He seemed to understand the feeling of strangeness for most of us in this new atmosphere of the army – the complete break with anything we had known previously. He wanted to temper this strangeness with the familiar. Despite the hard work, he tried to make our stay at Beaconsfield as pleasant as possible. To me, the three months I spent there were like the sort of university life I had missed out on. No-one turned up their noses at having spent time seeing *The Family Reunion*. On the contrary, at one interview I had to give my assessment of Eliot's *Cocktail Party* which I had been to see in London. Being so near, anyone asking for an evening pass to London to go to the Proms, or to visit the Open Air Theatre was immediately granted this. Wavell had numerous contacts and was able to bring many guest speakers to us, among whom were Alan Moorhead, author of two books on the Nile, and the novelist L. P. Hartley. We were encouraged to pursue any intellectual interests. We put on a production of *The Tempest* in which I played Caliban.

Major Wavell was a 'character'. We had been at Beaconsfield only two days when the seventy of us were assembled. We were told that he wanted to get to know all of us, that during our course he would have a chat with each one individually. He also wanted to make sure that he knew everyone by name. Thus he would go along the rows and name each one of us as far as he could. If he did not know or got a name wrong we should remain seated. Otherwise we could leave the hall. During the past two days I had not exchanged a single word with him, nor had I noticed that he had been aware of me. Of course, I realised he could not know my name. But as he went past person by person and the rows in front of me rapidly emptied, I began to have my doubts. When he came to me, he quite clearly said 'Levy'. I don't think there were more than half a dozen left seated by the time he had got through the whole company.

He knew of both my German and my Jewish origins. When it was time for my chat he took me to his room to show me a book. This had been sent to him after the war by the son of the German Army General Rommel. It is well known that Rommel always maintained that F.M. Wavell had been his most astute opponent, an assessment which he acknowledged in the book. Now Wavell very much wanted me to translate the part that referred to his father. Typically for him, he was intrigued by the reference to the only word he understood: 'whisky'.

He was a very charming man and we had a most interesting conversation. At the end he told me that in the present company he had found the most pleasant group of Jews he had ever come across, which seemed to surprise him greatly. I must stress that he was never anti-semitic and no doubt wanted to be encouraging to me. But there was this inbred feeling within him. I really could not take it amiss, though it amused me slightly. I saw him a number of times after I left the army, at reunions and suchlike events. Like all sons of famous fathers he had great difficulty in living up to expectations and was always striving to do so. Later on he served in Kenya at the time of the Mau-Mau troubles and – doubtless by being too brave once too often – was killed while on patrol. I attended a memorial service to him at the Tower. I shall always remember him with affection for trying and succeeding in making a difficult time for young people more acceptable.

The Army Educational Corps (A.E.C.) had only recently

acquired the additional title of Royal. Some said, rather cynically, still others wrily, for services to the Labour Party. It had become apparent that a great number of people in the Armed Forces had voted for the Labour Party during the 1945 election, which gave Labour for the first and almost last time a landslide victory. Many people felt this was due to the A.B.C.A. lectures given by members of the Educational Corps. A.B.C.A. stood for Army Bureau of Current Affairs and I am sure most of these lectures dealt with matters of interest in daily life and hopes for the future. However, I do not for a moment suppose that these young lecturers were as persuasive as all that. Towards the end of the war there were great expectations of a new era of change which people believed only a Labour government would deliver. Yet the idea that it was these A.B.C.A. lecturers, with their powerful pleading, who were responsible for the Labour victory in 1945 still persists. A few years ago, while my wife and I were on holiday in East Anglia, we met a very pleasant retired general. He insisted that that victory in 1945 was all the fault of those 'Welsh Pinkos' in the Educational Corps at that time (why Welsh I do not know!).

We had no sooner arrived at Beaconsfield than it was decided that National Service would be increased from 18 months to two years again. After three months' service, we found we had longer to serve now than when we had started. Major Wavell came round to all the barrack rooms to see how we were taking it and to ensure our morale would not suffer.

While we enjoyed the atmosphere of the camp we also had work to do. We had something called T.Ps (Teaching Practices). Each group of a dozen or fifteen had to decide on a course in English or Mathematics. The course was divided into the number of people in the group, so that each one of us had to give one lesson on that subject to the rest of the group. The object was to make the lesson exciting and keep the 'pupils' awake. I had been surprised at Winchester that the most popular reading materials were children's comics like the Dandy and Beano. Therefore in

93

my English lesson on inverted commas of reported speech I started with the balloon speech of 'Eggo the Ostrich' in the Beano. I showed how much easier it was to use these inverted commas than the cumbersome balloons. The whole thing was rather academic as once you have a proper class in front of you, you handle it quite differently anyway, as we were soon to find out.

Major Wavell decided that all of us would go to Aldershot for one week to work with other R.A.E.C. personnel who were already in the field. There was objection from higher up to this innovation, as it was feared we would become disillusioned too early by seeing what it was really like in practice, rather than what we had been taught in theory. I am not altogether sure whether they did not have a point. However, permission was granted and I found myself facing a group of soldiers for the first time. This was without the additional benefit of stripes on my sleeve. All R.A.E.C. personnel became sergeants once they had finished their course. However, I had the Aldershot R.A.E.C. sergeant in my class all the time to back me up, so my ordeal was not that bad. I returned to Beaconsfield without too many misgivings.

Over the Bank Holiday weekend we all got leave to go to our various homes. At the end of the holiday, as part of an initiative test, we had to make our way to the top of Snowdon by a certain time. We were to meet at Capel Curig and then make the ascent en masse.

I left Hampstead bright and early and took the tube to Stanmore, where I met up with a friend who had come from Wimbledon. From Stanmore we could start along the A5, which was a direct road to North Wales. At that time there was no such thing as a motorway, nor was it as dangerous then to catch a lift from passing traffic. However, there were far fewer cars on the road. Seventy people started more or less at the same time from all parts of Britain towards Snowdon. It was not too difficult to get a lift while we were all rather far apart. But as the seventy of us slowly gathered on North Wales, and cars got fewer, it became less easy. On

94

the last leg of the journey we often saw cars pass by with grinning faces of fellow soldiers waving at us.

Meanwhile the weather had deteriorated as well. It started raining heavily. By the time we arrived in Capel Curig the weather was so bad that Major Wavell had had to abandon his idea of camping out. He had found a church hall where we could get dry and spend the night. The next morning the rain had stopped but a terrible wind had got up. Indeed it was so stormy that the train, which takes the more lazy traveller to the top of Snowdon, had stopped its journeys.

We nevertheless went ahead. It got more and more difficult as we got higher. Towards the end we clambered along the railway track, which we knew was not being used. There was no view at the top as it was much too cloudy and we had our work cut out to get down again.

We had a week to spend there. Major Wavell encouraged us to think up our own schemes for the remaining days. Three of us had a plan for explorations well away from Capel Curig. We had our own bivouac tent and could stay away for three or four days. Major Wavell gave us his permission on two conditions: we had to phone in each evening and we had to promise to shave each morning. The three of us had a brilliant time exploring the countryside. The weather had also improved and we were sorry to leave what for me had been my first-ever visit to Wales.

The end of the training was fast approaching and we were to receive our sergeant stripes. Luckily there was only one R.T.U. (Returned To Unit). The statutory passing-out parade was preceded by the traditional passing-out party the previous night, which necessitated a number of passers-out being put in the centre of three rows to be kept in an upright position by colleagues on either side of them. Before this we received our postings. We could state our preference. The most sought after placing was one in Trieste. The lucky young man who got this posting never returned. He was killed when he was involved in a lorry accident over there.

A small number of people were sent to Malaya. They took part in quite dangerous patrols against Communist insurgents active there at that time.

The Educational Corps was very busy at that time for a number of reasons. During the war there had, for obvious reasons, been a great number of promotions in the ranks of the regular army. This did not always square with their academic achievements. In order to keep their non-commissioned rank, each person had to achieve at least the lowest of the three Army Certificates of Education. The top certificate was somewhere just below the level of School Certificate. Some of these men, who sometimes had been in the army for a great number of years and who were moreover advanced in years, must have found it rather degrading to be taught by young boys just out of school.

As a German speaker I fully expected to be sent to Germany in order to help our troops there improve their knowledge of the local language. For whatever reason, I was not sent there. Possibly because of my German connections, the authorities might have thought I was perhaps a likely target for blackmail by the other side. Or perhaps they did not trust me anyway. In any case, I got a posting to a Boys' Training Regiment in Yorkshire. As soon as I got there, just outside Beverley in what was then the East Riding, I got such a severe attack of shingles that I spent the first few weeks in the military hospital in York.

Beverley at that time was a beautiful small market town. It had its market square and regular market days, its crooked lanes and the beautiful Minster. The multiple stores had not yet taken over every High Street. Each county town still had its individuality. It is described by Winifred Holtby as the fictional county town, Flintonbridge, in her novel *South Riding*. Television had not yet reached the North of England and the numerous cinemas showed films which London had seen several years before.

Our camp, Victoria Barracks, was a mile or two outside Beverley, next to the East Yorkshire Regiment H.Q. It consisted of the usual nissen huts, the semi-cylindrical corrugated iron buildings, or wooden barracks. There were no brick buildings, except for the officers' quarters. It was a training regiment in the Signal Corps for boy soldiers. These were teenagers between 15 and $17^1/_2$ who spent their time here before joining adult regiments. The elite training centre for this age group was the Army Boys Apprentice School in Harrogate. I spent a few days there later on when I had to take some of my pupils to sit for their School Certificate examination. This was a properly run place where young men were taught, and could acquire, a trade as had been promised to them. In Beverley it was a completely different story. A large number of the boys were those who had been in trouble with the police. The juvenile courts, before which they had to appear, often gave them a choice of either being sent to a Borstal institution or joining the army where it was promised they would learn a trade. At Beverley there were few facilities for being taught a trade. There was a large contingent of R.A.E.C. personnel apart from some Signals people, but the teenagers, who had left school at 14, mostly resented 'going back to school'.

There were three main types of boys. Firstly there were the intelligent ones who now had a chance, which they had never had before, of passing examinations and even getting some passes in School Certificates. G.C.E. and G.C.S.E. were still very much in the future. It was a pleasure to teach them and to encourage their enthusiasm. This being only a few years after the end of the war, when many children's education had been frequently interrupted, the second group consisted of people who could neither read nor write. They were mightily embarrassed by this fact. They would often go to the cinema and see the same film again, as they could not read what was being shown and were too ashamed to ask anyone. They could not even write a letter home. This group also was eager to learn and were most grateful as they slowly began to be able to write a few words. However, the vast majority of the people, who had left school at 14 being able to read and write moderately well, who thought that they knew it all, were highly resentful of being made to learn more. They did have to acquire one of the three Certificates of Army Education to be able later on to take up a course for a trade. Even once they got the lowest certificate the trade training never materialised and at age 18 most of them were passed onto the R.A.S.C. (the Service Corps).

The boys came from all over the UK. Many came from the Glasgow Gorbals district, which at that time was quite a slum. There were people from the South of England. One boy even came from the Channel Islands. His name was LeFeuvre, which he insisted was pronounced Lefever. Some people came from broken homes, from divorced parents, some had suffered mental and physical abuse. Some of these young boys were frightened by this sudden and unusual strict discipline. Others were extremely homesick. The army is not very well able to deal with these youngsters. A number of them disappeared, they went A.W.O.L. They were mostly confused children who needed what we now call social workers. What they got instead were young men, hardly older than the people they were supposed to help, with no experience of looking after cases like this. There was no course of social work at the Army School of Education nor at any other Army establishment as far as I know. Not only were we teachers, but nannies as well, sometimes with very disturbed youngsters to deal with. I know myself how difficult the situation was at times. How much I could believe of the stories I had to listen to. How much I could do within Army regulations. How to supply advice about situations I had never come across before. Sadly to realise what a pitiable future was beckoning most of these young people.

We got plenty of advice from above about the teaching. Not that we necessarily agreed or even found it possible to comply with it. We were told to get away from the blackboard. Yes, we said, but how in mathematics? Go out and let them measure the parade ground, they said. Right, what else? Silence! What in English? Don't answer their questions, we were told, let them look it up in an encyclopaedia. This was for people who were unable to spell. Get them out of the classroom, we were told. I did try whenever possible. We had a good day out, watching the boat builders along the river Hull.

Once I tried my own experiment outside the classroom. The lesson was on reported speech, both spoken and written. I decided to enact a motor car accident outside the classroom, with the pupils playing the different parts. Afterwards everyone had to write and verbally report his own version of the accident. The only trouble was that my classroom was very near the Company H.Q. The full-blooded acting of the class soon brought out the C.S.M. (Company Sergeant Major) from his office, wanting to know what was happening. The new method of teaching, he was told. He replied that the new method should be confined to the inside of the classroom.

In addition to the teaching the sergeants were also responsible for a number of barrack rooms and their inmates. The principle the army works on is to divest oneself of as much responsibility as possible. This is achieved by diverting the responsibility onto someone else and the method of doing so is the signature. Whatever the responsibility a signature is obtained from someone else. There was a certain amount of furniture in the barrack rooms. The Q.M. (Quarter Master) issued these items and obtained a signature. From time to time there were inspections of the barrack rooms to check on the inventories.

The barrack rooms were very cold during the winter months. In the years after the war the country was still very short of fuel, so that the coal used in the iron stoves of these barracks often ran out. But the boys were very cold. So often part of or even a whole wooden chair or bedside table, for the use of, would be cut up and fed into the stove. This played havoc with the inventories at the time of inspection. A very simple remedy was found. The first two barrack rooms to be inspected were fully prepared as per their inventory through borrowing items from other rooms.

When Room One had been inspected, and while it was the turn of Room Two to be checked, Room Three was replenished with its missing items from Room One and so on down the line. Thus every inventory was found to be correct and the Q.M. or his deputy left fully satisfied.

These were some of the more amusing moments. But time and again I thought sadly of what the future held for most of these boys, who had signed up to serve in the army for a great number of years, without realising fully what they were letting themselves in for. The only way they could get out of this situation was either by buying themselves out, which was beyond their means, or by behaving in such an atrocious way that they would get a dishonourable discharge, which would be on their record for the rest of their lives. In order to achieve even this, they would have to spend some time in the Military Prison at Colchester. Having once been to that place – as a visitor not as an inmate, may I quickly add – it is something I do not wish on anyone.

My two years' service finally came to an end. These two years seemed very long indeed. Was it of benefit to anyone? I cannot flatter myself that it benefited the country in any way. As to myself, as time passes one looks back on it with a certain nostalgia. As I said at the very beginning, it certainly brought me in contact with groups of people I would never have met otherwise. I suppose it gave me a certain maturity. Did anyone benefit by my being there? I really do not think so, though I like to imagine that, like Major Wavell at Beaconsfield, I made the time a little easier for some of the boys at Beverley.

12

DISCOVERING SHAKESPEARE

As I spent almost my first ten years in Germany it is not surprising that rather than Shakespeare it was Goethe, Schiller and Lessing that provided me with my introduction to the classics. My uncle being an actor and my family interested in literature, it naturally followed that I had the German plays read to me from an early age. As soon as I could read myself, I started on my own on plays like *Wilhelm Tell*, *Maria Stuart*, *Die Jungfrau von Orleans* and *Minna von Barnhelm*. But Shakespeare, even though considered by many Germans as *unser Shakespeare* (our Shakespeare), did not come to my notice until much later. I have had discussions on several occasions with German-speaking people who have quite seriously advanced the proposition that Shakespeare in a German translation is far superior to the original: *Eine Umdichtung* – a reinterpretation they maintain. Needless to say they usually had not read the original.

I do remember reading parts of *Romeo and Juliet* in German, because at one time my uncle participated in a production of that play. After I had been in this country less than a year, all the pupils in the school I attended at the time were assembled to watch a scene from a Shakespeare play being performed by the top class. I didn't understand a word of it. I can only remember a sword fight and have always therefore assumed it must have been from the end of *Hamlet*.

The first Shakespeare play I ever saw – in fact the first play I ever saw on a professional stage – was *Macbeth,* the plot of which I knew. Soon after I saw the Robert Atkins production of *A Midsummer Night's Dream* at the Westminster Theatre. I suddenly realised that Shakespeare could also be funny and found the Pyramus and Thisbe scenes at the end of the play hilarious.

Slowly I began to get to know Shakespeare. *Macbeth* was to become my matriculation play. We also read other plays at school: *Julius Caesar* and *Richard II* and despite all their endeavours, by making the readings as dull as possible, none of the schoolmasters could kill my interest in Shakespeare.

During the war years, at the Old Vic Company's productions at the New Theatre and at other places I saw some of the tragedies and history plays. But it was always my ambition to get to Stratford-on-Avon. I still have a postcard that my friend Karl-Heinz Guttmann sent me during the war while he was visiting Stratford. It had fired my imagination and the yearning to get there grew with the years. For many reasons – the Nazi period in Germany, wartime conditions, movement restrictions for aliens, lack of money – I had never been on a holiday, apart from visiting relatives. All my school holidays during the war were spent at home. When therefore I started earning money I decided immediately that my first proper holiday would be spent in Stratford. This I did and went there all on my own.

The whole business was much more complicated than it would be nowadays, especially for someone who had never made such arrangements before. Where should I stay? My aunt, who was an actress, when on tour used to write to the local police station of a town to ask for addresses where she could lodge. I did the same and the Stratford police gave me a number of bed and breakfast accommodations of which I chose one to stay for the eight days or so. Railways were still running in 1947, but there was no direct line to Stratford-on-Avon. One had to change trains at Leamington. Although Stratford was already a tourist attraction at that time, it had not yet become the magnet for visitors that it is nowadays. The season of plays was much shorter, just during the few summer months.

The Royal Shakespeare Company was still in the dim, distant future, some thirteen years away. The theatre was known as the Shakespeare Memorial Theatre and thus the company was the Shakespeare Memorial Company, with no London outlet. During the war it had functioned often under the direction of Robert Atkins. But this was the second season under the control of Barry Jackson, the founder of the Birmingham Rep which had a very high reputation. He had introduced several innovations, bringing two stars from the London stage, Robert Harris and Beatrix Lehman and engaging several newcomers, among them unknowns like Donald Sinden.

The town itself was not overcrowded with visitors even in the middle of July, nor was it overrun with cars seeking the few parking places available. Stratford was one of England's many market towns with its regular market days in the square. It just so happened that England's most famous writer had been born there. But already its citizens were beginning to realise the marketable value of its most illustrious son with Shakespeare trinkets as souvenirs, Shakespeare Tea Shoppes to drop into of an afternoon and a Shakespeare Garage for those lucky enough to have twentieth century forms of transport. But one could still walk comfortably on uncrowded pavements and breathe in the atmosphere of Britain's literary heritage.

A taxi took me to my accommodation. Quickly I unpacked and went over Clopton Bridge to view the town and look at the theatre. Although I had booked for most nights – rather extravagantly, back stalls at 4/6d each (22½p) – I did not have seats for the first night and got a queuing stool for the gallery that night. The play that evening was *Twelfth Night*. I had never seen it before nor did I know it. There is something unusual in coming to a Shakespeare play for the first time when his plays are so well known. But there must be someone at every performance

103

for whom it is a completely new experience. People do not usually come to Shakespeare for the plot, yet each time there are people in the audience for whom development of the story is full of surprises. And there is something exciting in seeing a Shakespeare play for the first time. My first encounter with *Twelfth Night* was unforgettable. Even after nearly 50 years I can remember the production by Walter Hudd. He introduced the entire cast in shadow play. He inverted the first two scenes – as I was to learn later.

Beatrix Lehman said, 'What country friends is this?' and we were off.

Here was the wonderful story of twins lost at sea – the girl disguising herself as a boy, who has women falling in love with her/him. The mistaken identities, the absurdity of the planted letter and of the cross gartering and the final reconciliation. I don't know whether I appreciated the poetry or whether I was too busy following the plot lines.

This was the season when a new young director who had created quite a stir in the fringe theatres of London emerged for the first time in Stratford. Barely in his twenties, Peter Brook directed a production of *Romeo and Juliet* that was full of the heat and sweat of southern Italy. It was a very exciting production using the stage and auditorium to the fullest extent. At this time the theatre at Stratford did not have a revolving stage but one that would slide from side to side into the wings. The theory was that scenery could be moved and refitted on one side off stage, while the other side was being acted upon, thus avoiding numerous intervals for the necessary scene changes. Unfortunately the backstage space was not very wide, so that part of the sliding stage had to curl in order that it could slide up on the wall. This rather defeated the object of the exercise as nothing could be built on that part of the stage that was up the wall. Peter Brook's set consisted of an enormous house and balcony. It was so vast that though it stopped at the very edge before the stage rose on the wall, it could still be seen in the auditorium throughout the performance. The Romeo and Juliet were played by two young actors, Laurence Payne and Daphne Slater, who for the first time in many years were near the ages of the two characters in the play. Mercutio was played by an actor for whom a bright future was predicted called Paul Scofield.

Most mornings there were lectures by Dr Ifor Evans on the play to be seen that evening. I went to them and found them most stimulating so that I felt I had to study the plays more. This was the great difference between the lectures and school. Here was someone who loved Shakespeare, loved to talk and teach about him and examine the text, whereas in schools very often it is a matter solely of preparing pupils to answer the kind of questions expected in exam papers without conveying the magic of the poetry and the wonderful evocation of the characterisation.

I did all the tourist bits – the Birthplace, the Church, the School, Anne Hathaway's Cottage. It was quite an experience and a great success. In fact I could look back on it with such joy, that it was natural that years later I suggested to my young bride that we should go to Stratford-on-Avon on our honeymoon. But still at that time it was lonely and new. Despite the fact that I was always eager to hear and read about the latest Middlesex Cricket score – it was the year of Middlesex's miracle season with those terrible twins Dennis Compton and Bill Edrich scoring centuries galore in almost every match – I was alone most of the time in strange surroundings.

I came down in the morning to an English breakfast, which I was not used to. What was a nice Jewish boy to make of cornflakes and bacon and eggs. Even at that time there was an abundance of restaurants serving lunches every day. However I always chose the same one and usually the same menu. I became so well known there, they suggested they reserve a table for me. However I did not want to commit myself. All that was of so little importance. Every night it was the theatre that was the stimulating experience. The other plays during the season included *Richard II*, which I had done at school, *The Merchant of Venice* and *The Tempest*. I had missed another play I did not know: *Love's Labour's Lost* in what I believe was a good production. However I was to come across it for the first time two years later at the Old Vic in another exhilarating production with Michael Redgrave as Berowne.

Though I had often wanted to discuss the performances I really spoke to no-one until the last night. While queuing for the gallery I met a young man from Coventry and had long conversations with him before, during and after the play. It was the sort of conversation I often had with a London friend, Henry Young, after a concert or a play, when we were full of new impressions which had to be debated. I regretted that I could not have met this young man rather at the beginning than at the end of my holiday.

Alas, the excitement of seeing and discovering a Shakespeare play for the first time is something that can never be repeated. There is however one compensation in later years. This I have found most rewarding – a second chance in life that otherwise one seldom gets. The pleasure of introducing a favourite play or a much loved book to one's children gives one the opportunity to participate vicariously in their joy of discovery. As one watches their faces the years seem to fade away.

13

GRIM FAIRYTALE

There are some strange stories about – stranger than fiction people say, because if writers were to invent them no-one would believe them. There are some stories with bitter-sweet happy endings. This is one of those.

My wife Lilian was born in London. In fact while our two children still lived at home it was a standing joke that I was the only foreigner in the house. She came into the world two weeks before the 1939-45 war broke out. As soon as Hitler invaded Poland, Lilian's mother left her sister's family, took her daughter and decided they should rejoin her husband, who was still in Holland. They caught one of the last passenger planes out of Croydon airport on Sunday, September 3rd. As German Jews, Lilian's parents had left Nazi Germany for the comparative safety of Holland. Holland had been neutral in the first World War – there was no reason to believe it would not remain so this time round. Thousands of Jews sheltering in Holland made this mistake. Once the Germans invaded Holland the anti-Jewish policy of the Nazis was also enacted there. Lilian and her parents were taken to the Dutch Westerbork concentration camp and onto the notorious Bergen-Belsen. Lilian's status of being British-born was no help. Both Lilian's parents died in the camp. Lilian miraculously survived. At the end of the war she was returned to Westerbork and then to an orphanage. At the age of not yet six she had experienced

107

more than others in a lifetime.

Lilian's aunt had survived the war in London. Now she hoped to have news of the members of her family caught in Europe by the war. Lilian in her orphanage was the only one to survive.

Lilian returned to England in 1946 and came to stay with her aunt. As her husband was sick, the aunt decided to put Lilian out for adoption. A Jewish couple – former residents of Berlin – adopted her. They gave her the sort of life and education her aunt might have found difficult to provide. Lilian grew up in this doctor's house. We met, got married, had two children and Lilian's adoptive mother, now widowed, came to live with us.

All this time Lilian still saw her aunt, but could never find out anything about her past. The aunt would not talk or did not know – no-one else knew. And for Lilian, her life had begun at the age of six, with a large void before then. Lilian's adoptive mother died. And when Lilian's aunt fell ill, she looked after her for several years until the aunt died too.

And then, in the true tradition of fairy tales, Lilian found a treasure – but what a treasure: not money, nor jewels, but letters. The aunt had never been able to throw anything away. All the letters she had ever received had been carefully stored. And though she never talked about the past, this past – Lilian's past – was revealed in the correspondence that was found. Among the letters that were discovered was one from Mr Birnbaum, the man who had brought Lilian back from Bergen-Belsen to Holland.

In the letter, actually addressed to another relative in the USA, he described in detail some of the life in the camp and the journey back to Holland. He had traced family members of the orphan children who had returned with him. Thus Lilian had been reunited with her aunt.

Who was this Mr Birnbaum, where was he and was he still alive? Another letter was found, written by the aunt years later, to Mr Birnbaum to inform him of what had happened to his charge and how she had fared. This letter, sent to

Holland, had been returned to the sender unopened, with the message, 'Gone to Israel'.

Where, when and how? Like a detective in a novel Lilian went to work. The sole possible source of help would be at Yad Vashem in Jerusalem, the memorial site to the Holocaust, which kept documentation not only on the six million victims, but also on the survivors. The letter was sent and information asked for. A reply came which told us that there was indeed a Mr Birnbaum, a survivor of Bergen-Belsen, living in Israel. However, his address could not be revealed. Lilian's request would be forwarded to him and if he felt he wanted to reply direct he could do so. Would he feel so inclined?

Days passed until there was a reply from Mr Birnbaum. Yes, he knew Lilian – though he remembered her as Lily – the youngest one of his charges and the only one he had been unable to trace since her departure to England. He was delighted to have traced her at last.

And as this is a sort of fairy tale, Lilian's aunt in her will had also left her a small sum of money, but just large enough to pay for her, me and our two children to go on our first trip to Israel to our meeting with Mr Birnbaum.

One can never relive the excitement of one's first visit to Israel, though the thrill of first seeing the view of Jerusalem on the road from the airport is renewed each time.

But Israel for the first time is something special, so much to see, so many people to meet. Many of our relatives, whom we had seen in London, were now able to show us their land. We saw Jerusalem with its Western Wall, we saw Haifa with its Carmel. And we also went to Nahariya, because that is where Mr and Mrs Birnbaum lived at the time. So many new encounters and this special meeting with people who had known Lilian as a little child and about whom we had known nothing barely a year ago.

I still remember the four of us travelling on the bus from Haifa to Nahariya – each one of us with our own thoughts. Nahariya is a charming little town – the German town, because so many from that country settled there. A town

109

right by the sea and the Birnbaum's house right on the sea-shore, so that one can hear the gentle lapping of the waves.

We rang the bell and were welcomed by a gentle little old couple – the pair were in their eighties now. We came in as strangers but not for long.

These were now the people who had known Lilian longer than anyone else, who had been with her at the time she lost her parents. It was an amazing story we learned and a unique experience for Lilian, whose dim recollections of camp life she had never been able to have confirmed.

There had been eight Birnbaums – the couple had six children – and all of them had been in Bergen-Belsen. There had been many children swarming about the barracks and finally Mr. Birnbaum, a former teacher, had asked and been given permission to look after them during the day. The place he was given was the mortuary where the dead bodies were kept – those who had died of starvation or disease, those who had died too soon before they could be transported to the gas chambers of Auschwitz. He started a little school in those surroundings. It was Lilian's father, realising his end was near, who asked Mr Birnbaum to look after Lilian and gave him such details about relatives that would be useful if any of them ever got out of that hell-hole.

By a miracle they were saved. As the Allies got nearer, the Nazis, trying to hide their tracks, moved them in trains further to the East to destroy the evidence. They were shunted to and fro and the train was attacked by Allied bombers, who assumed it to be a German troop train. At one point the bombing got so bad that they thought they could not survive. One little boy, true to the lessons he had been taught by Mr Birnbaum, asked him whether now was the time to say the *Sh'ma*, the Hebrew prayer.

Finally, released by the Russians, the Birnbaums made their way back to Holland with more than 50 children including their own six.

All the nightmares, all the memories of that time were confirmed.These were not dreams, not fantasies, but the dreadful memories of a four- and five-year-old: the wooden

110

slats made into four bunks round a central pole and the same arrangement four feet up; any rags one could find for blankets. The food once a day consisting of a piece of turnip floating in its own water plus a hunk of hard, black bread. The washing arrangements – rarely permitted – were shower rooms a very long walk away. And the time Lilian remembered that a lady told her that her parents were dead. That lady was Mrs Birnbaum.

So many years ago, so much to find out. The Birnbaums had sought information about Lilian, but her name had been changed because of the adoption. And all the time Mr Birnbaum's children in Jerusalem were friends with one of Lilian's adoptive cousins who also lived there and whom she had seen many times, who had in fact stayed with us on one of his London visits.

A real miracle. All these children had been saved by the Birnbaums and looked after and found homes for, once it was realised that most of their parents had perished. Lilian tried to state her gratitude. After all, they had saved her life.

Birnbaum replied simply, 'God saved your life. I was merely his instrument'.

After all that obscene wickedness, after all that evil, to keep one's faith: that is the true miracle.

14

THE CHOICE

It is as well to admit straight away that both my wife, Lilian, and I had grave doubts about having the 1991 Anne Frank Exhibition at Belsize Square Synagogue, let alone participating in it ourselves.

Our doubts were manifold: it had taken us years to go to the Anne Frank House. When we were finally in Amsterdam we had been shocked by some of the comments in the visitors' book – by their insensitivity and misunderstandings. They seemed to show the wrong attitude with which many of the visitors came to the House and how often they had left with little understanding of what had happened. We were perturbed by the sensationalism, in the worst meaning of that word, that had so often been seen on programmes on television and in the cinema. We had avoided all this – if it had to be told it should be told as it really was. In any case, it did not have to be told to us. We knew about it at first hand.

We discussed long and hard whether we should participate. This would be reopening old wounds, picking at sores that we hoped had left us, revealing intimate events about ourselves and our families that we had hoped that with the passing of time we could eventually try to forget about altogether. I believe we have a right to put aside all these things, to forget and to live a new life without bringing up these memories of 50 years ago. And I still believe that everyone has that right. But we also have a choice – and that word 'choice' appeared and followed me and followed the groups I led throughout the weeks of the exhibition.

It was our choice – once we had heard that a number of visiting schools would need guiding – to join the exhibition. It was our choice to give personal documents – some of the most painful letters and photographs we possess – that would be displayed there. And it had been our choice – by a true touch of irony – sometime before, coincidentally, that we had decided for rather personal reasons to spend a week in Berlin, which just happened to be the third week of the exhibition. Nothing could have given the past more immediacy.

To say one was worried, unsure, even frightened, would all be true. It was not only the possibility of having groups of unruly children to take around; most people would be able to cope with that. I was always conscious of young people's attention span, of the differing ages of the groups and the adjustment that had to be made for each individual group. But most of my worries were about myself and how I would cope, reliving my life of 50 years ago in front of strangers.

Some people maintained it would be some kind of therapy for the guides: if conducting people around the exhibition taught me to understand these events – and myself in them – somewhat better, it was therapeutic. If it was meant to lessen the pain of what had happened to me and my generation, it was a great failure.

'We all have a choice,' was what I told my groups.

And it was my choice, immediately after I had introduced myself, found out how much, if anything, they knew about Anne Frank and explained something about the peculiarly apt nature of this Synagogue to house this exhibition, that I would start with my picture of a nine-year-old, months before he left Germany.

And as I looked at myself 50 years ago and looked into the faces of the children, I began to understand something of myself. There they were, looking at a picture of me at a fairly similar age to theirs. And I suddenly realised how different my youth had been to theirs. It is always said time is a great healer. Unfortunately I have never found it so – certainly not regarding the events of the Nazi period. On the contrary: over the years these events have become more menacing, more frightening, more horrendous. And looking at those mostly cheerful faces and myself at their age, the differences began to fall into place. I had spent the first ten years of my life under most extraordinary conditions. I had experienced in my first ten years events and happenings that none of them – we trust – would ever experience in a lifetime. But to me as a child it had been the norm, unpleasant no doubt, but something that had to be accepted because I had never known anything different. It is only with the realisation in adult life how different, how extraordinary, how vile all this had been, that I can acknowledge and understand the whole revulsion of these events. And this understanding brings with it the pain that does not ameliorate but increases with the years.

And returning to Berlin, where now life is as normal as it will ever be, visiting places I knew, reviving painful memories, having myself lived through most of it, I – who had been there at the time – I still cannot understand how it could all have happened.

There is a choice, we always stressed. My main object in explaining to young people what happened so many years before any of them were born was to find for them the relevance it may have today – to draw the analogy of what is happening in the world in their own lifetime.

I start with my picture because the analogy immediately becomes obvious. The Identity Card – the additional Jewish forename, the big red J stamped on the card. It is the same categorising of people as it was until recently in South Africa into white, coloured and black.

I judge their attention span and I spend most of the time on the outer ring of the exhibition: *The Rise of Hitler, to 1938.* How could these things have happened in Germany – what led up to them and could in similar situations other

114

minorities be treated in such a way? The parallels crowd themselves upon you all the time. I ensured that there was always sufficient time to view the final section of what is happening in the world today. And there are so many events taking place in tandem. It is not just South Africa, not just opinion polls in Austria, not just M. Le Pen in France, not just David Duke, the former Grand Wizard of the Ku Klux Klan, who hoped to become Governor of the State of Louisiana. He did not make it, but collected over 700,000 votes in the attempt – 700,000 votes which is more than half the white population in the State of Louisiana. Not only these events, but what is happening in Britain at the same time. I could not help but compare the difficulties that are being put in the way of today's refugees – not believing that they are genuine refugees, as we and our parents were not believed. Being refused and sent back to their countries of origin to be tortured or worse, as the ships full of Jewish refugees were turned back 50 years ago.

There are many parallels and many choices. The Germans had a choice, the Dutch had a choice – it was the Jews who had very little choice. From the earliest Hitler years they tried to find safe havens but no country would take them in in sufficient numbers. And today's children in their later life will have choices to make. I hope that something of what they saw will remain with them, so that when the time comes to make their own choices, remembering this exhibition will help them to make the right choice.

It was an agonising decision to participate, which led quite literally to many sleepless nights and nightmares before, during and after the exhibition. It was our choice.

I quote from one reluctant witness in the book *The Last Seven Months of Anne Frank*: 'For more than 40 years I had pushed that aside because I really wanted to live normally and I didn't want to talk about it any more.'

Some of us will never be able to recount these painful episodes in our lives. We must respect their wishes. The choice is theirs.

APPENDIX

TRANSLATIONS OF LETTERS:
LONDON-BERLIN-LONDON, Summer 1939

Letter from Herbert in Berlin to Uncle Joszi and Aunt Hanna, dated 20.2.39.

My Dear Ones,

I got a note-pad today, that is why I am writing to you today. I hope the permit comes soon. I am looking forward to being able to travel to England. At our school half the class is registered to go to England with a Kindertransport and no-one has left so far.

For today lots of love.

Your nephew Herbert.

Postcard to parents on the train to Holland, 20.6.39.

Dear Parents,

Am happy on the train. Can't write any more, it's too bumpy on the train; will write more later. Still no station. Now the first station. Can't write more, must catch the post.

Regards

Herbert.

Postcard from Harwich, 21.6.39.

Dear Parents,

I have about an hour's time. Forgive me for not writing to you from Hook that card went to Karlsruhe [to my grandmother]. *I and nine other children are sitting in a room in the Customs*

116

House. *I am very happy and am well. I wasn't seasick on the boat. Lots of love and kisses.*
    Herbert

Postcard 22.6.39.
Dear Parents, dear Grandparents,
    Today I have had no post from you, am very worried. Did you get the permit yet? Tomorrow week I shall go to school for the first time. Today I have rearranged Uncle Joszi's shop in the house. Ink costs 2d, pencil with rubber 1d, etc.
    For today lots of love and kisses,
    Herbert.

Letter dated 23.6.39.
Received a card from you today and was very happy to have news of you. I shall now describe my journey: our accompanying leaders were Messrs. Hirschfeld, Schaefer and Englaender. The first stop after Berlin was Stendal, then Hannover, then Osnabrück, then Bentheim. Aunt Anna only looked through the door [this is a reference to Nazi control at the border]. *We went via Rotterdam. I wasn't seasick on the boat, but at home. We had breakfast on the ship.*
    Love and kisses,
    Herbert.

Letter dated 26.6.39.
Today we received the letter with keys to the suitcase. I don't know how we are to fetch the suitcase from the station. Yesterday, Sunday, we went with Mr Carr's car to Windsor Castle from where we sent you a picture postcard. It is very nice here even if the weather is bad. It'll start to rain any minute now. We have a lovely garden. I play in it all day, water the flowers, weed the paths and so on. Everyone calls me 'gardener'. The gardener also administers Uncle Joszi's business in the house. Each day I collect 1/-, 6d, etc. I have already seen the room that you, dear Parents, and I shall get [when you

117

arrive here]. *It has a lot of sun and there is a built-in locker. The room that we have now will be for the grandparents. It is very suitable for Grandad, because it is on the ground floor* [basement, actually]. *Next year we shall build an arbour, then Grandad can always sit in the garden. I have a lot more to write but the others want to have their say.*

Card dated 27.6.39.
Received the two reply cards today. Meanwhile you will have received my detailed letter. Today was the first fine day. We were out in the sun the whole day. It was very jolly. Tomorrow I shall go with Aunt Dora [special name for Hanna whose mother in Germany could have been at risk from the Nazis] *to the cinema, perhaps to a park the day after. You will like it very much over here. It is very nice and I never want to leave.*

Letter dated 28.6.39.
Received the reply card last night. Why don't you send a letter? I have only had one so far. Yesterday we collected the furniture from Posner [our former doctor in Berlin. I was the page at his wedding. They were in London before moving on to Australia.] *We have already furnished the room. It contains: 1 writing desk which will take the place of the one you had to leave behind, dear Dad. 1 washstand that Dr. Posner had in his surgery. 2 chairs, 1 armchair, pictures. Curtains are already hanging at the window. In the market* [Caledonian Market] *everything is cheap and good. If you are able to bring anything, I suggest bedding, couch, bookcase, perhaps also chairs, crockery, pans, large pots, etc. There is a built-in locker in the room. There is a wonderful view from the room. Also, dear Grandparents, you will be able to look into the garden. You must not despair, you will get the permit. When you are here you will see for yourselves and we shall be able to explain it better to you. Many people came here with loud mouths:- 'Once I have arrived . . .' and now they droop their heads and are miserable. As regards the cuisine, I am well looked after and Grandad will be able to eat 1 lb. butter and ten eggs and more,*

118

every day. [Food was already rationed in Germany at that time].

Card dated 30.6.39.
Just now received your card of the 29th. I wrote to Karlsruhe on the very first day. Tomorrow - because now it is 10 o'clock at night - I will write to Karlsruhe. I am dead tired and will go to bed now. I would have been in bed long ago, only we visited Jacoby.

Letter dated 4.7.39.
Don't be angry that I did not add a note to yesterday's letter. It was because I was away. Aunt Lotti wrote to us that you also got work permits with your travel permits. Do write yes or no. I have already been to the cinema twice. You will feel great here. The grandparents need not think that I have forgotten them. Dear Grandad, please don't cry, but keep your strength so that you can come here. Today the weather is wonderful and I am writing in the garden. In the meantime we went into town to look for an apartment for Aunt Lotti and Uncle Fred. Unfortunately, we don't know how much it will cost. If you don't want to, you don't have to bring any furniture. There is of course a built-in locker in the room and one can get beds very cheaply here. We have seen to it that everything is on hand for you to wash, sit, write and so on.

Letter dated 7.7.39.
Dear Mum,
I'm writing to congratulate you today, as I don't want to write tomorrow [the Sabbath]. *So, dear Mum, today I congratulate you for the first time from far away. Nevertheless, the good wishes are as heartfelt as always. If perhaps you aren't here yet for my birthday, then you will definitely be here the following month. So don't cry, soon we shall see each other again. Look forward to your birthday and think that 39 years ago you were born in London and this year you will return. You can go by tram for one penny to your birthplace. Many congratulations.* [I continued to the rest of the family].

119

My dear ones,
Received your letter last night. You don't have to bring the
bedroom furniture with you, nor the chaise longue. We could
certainly use the gas cooker very well. Next to the room is a small
area that one can use as a kitchen. The luggage has still not
arrived.

Letter dated 12.7.39.
All the sleeping arrangements have been seen to. What they are
will be a surprise. Your bedroom furniture doesn't matter any more.
It would be good if you could bring the two couches. Should these
not have arrived, arrangements for this eventuality have also been
made. Today is Thursday. Yesterday it was three weeks since I
arrived here. Really, how quickly time passes. I feel as if I was born
here. Yesterday I went to Woolworth with Aunt Hanna. I bought a
gardening trowel and two plants. You see, Uncle Joszi gives me 6d
each week. I've already got a savings box. Friday evenings I light
the candles and make Kiddush [blessing over the wine]. You
won't want to leave here. Grandad, you must not despair. In a
short time all of us will be sitting here. Even if we have to economise
and cut down on things and Uncle Joszi has to work very hard, we
will just have to make a go of it. [My grandfather died on 17th
July. Shortly afterwards we received a communication from
a Jewish Aid Society that my parents were about to receive
permission for entry into this country].

Card, late July
As Uncle Joszi wrote to you, we got the news [of the permit]
today. How happy I was. You, dear Mum, don't have to complain
any more: 'With other people it takes two months'. It has taken you
three.
[My parents left Berlin on 15th August and arrived, via
Hamburg and Southampton, in London on 18th August].

Postcard from my grandmother to all of us, after saying good-bye to my parents in Berlin. (15th August, 1939)

Dear Children,

Lo [Her nephew's non-Jewish wife] *has just come from the station to fetch me and we shall go soon. I'm feeling rather depressed.*

Lots of love,
your Mother.

[Her niece-in-law added]

My Dear Ones,

Just now Mulli & Arthur [my parents] *have left and I am now with Aunt Jettchen* [my grandmother] *to get her safely to Emserstrasse* [where my grandmother's sister lived]. *In the meantime we received your letter ...*

Yours Lo.

Final Red Cross letter dated 13/7/1942, limited to 25 words, from my grandmother Stein before deportation to Theresienstadt and Auschwitz.

Am well except for my leg. Will depart tomorrow with Aunt Hannah. Will remain there. Will not come back. Don't worry. Love to all.

MISHPOCHOLOGY

LEVY/DREIFUSS Family Tree

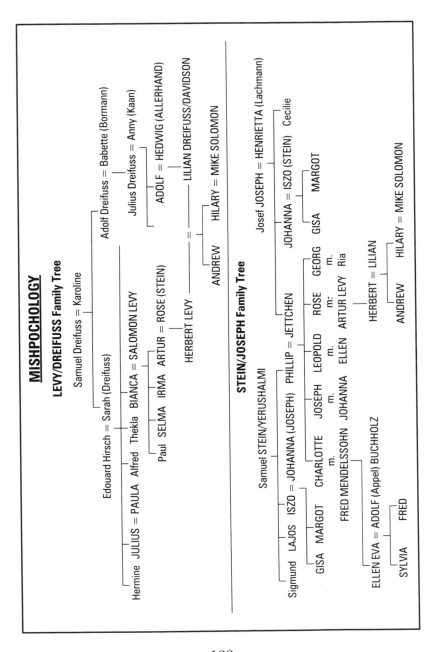

STEIN/JOSEPH Family Tree